D0207472

Library of Peasant Studies No. 4

THE RUSSIAN PEASANT

1920 and 1984

The Russian Peasant
1920 and 1984

Edited by

R. E. F. SMITH

FRANK CASS & CO. LTD.

First published 1977 in Great Britain by
FRANK CASS & COMPANY LIMITED
Gainsborough House, Gainsborough Road,
London E11 1RS, England

and in the United States of America by
FRANK CASS & COMPANY LIMITED
c/o International Scholarly Book Services Inc.
Box 555, Forest Grove, Oregon 97116

Copyright © 1977   Frank Cass & Co. Ltd.

ISBN   0 7146 3078 0

This group of studies first appeared in a Special Issue on
The Russian Peasant 1920 and 1984 of *The Journal of
Peasant Studies*, Volume 4 Number 1, published by
Frank Cass and Company Limited.

Printed in Great Britain by Chapel River Press, Andover, Hants.

Contents

Editors' Introduction

Of all the world's peasantries, perhaps none has been the object of such close scrutiny, such heated debate, or such cataclysmic change as the Russian. It would be difficult to overestimate the significance for students of peasant societies of the investigations and the large quantity of statistics which they yielded; of the differing views of the nature, characteristics, and likely destiny of Russia's peasants; of the transformations that were wrought in Russia's countryside from the emancipation of the serfs in 1861 to the experiments of the post-Revolution years and, ultimately, the collectivisation that was decreed in 1929. To this day the statistical procedures employed in the *zemstvo* censuses are of considerable interest to those who are faced with the task of gathering data in the countryside of poor countries; the formulations of the different and fundamentally opposed participants in the great debate are used as paradigms by those who study contemporary poor countries, the issues they contested fiercely are still contested, and the very vocabulary used has become the verbal currency of our time; and the changes engendered are examined for clues as to the institutional changes which are appropriate or possible in agrarian society.

We are fortunate to be able to publish in this book, edited by R. E. F. Smith, material never before translated into English—by Gorky, Bol'shakov and Chayanov—which throws fresh light upon some of the major issues of the Russian debate: upon both the widely divergent views of intellectuals towards Russia's peasantry and the realities of the Russian countryside. This material is yet further evidence of the richness and the diversity of the response to the Russian experience.

EDITORS, *The Journal of Peasant Studies*

Introduction*

R. E. F. Smith

In nineteenth-century Russia there had been an evolving tradition among intellectuals of sympathy for and understanding of the peasants. This included the Slavophil attitudes of the 1840s, stressing national features understood in a romantic and religious fashion, and then, a generation later, the Populist movement with its ardent, but ill-founded, desire to 'go to the people'. Greater understanding and increasing realism were achieved by participation in the *zemstva,* those local councils organised in much of European Russia after the emancipation of the serfs in 1861. Many thousands of educated men and women gradually came to have close knowledge of the Russian countryside when they were employed by *zemstva* as doctors, teachers, agricultural officers, veterinary surgeons, statisticians and so on. This was the proving ground of many Socialist Revolutionaries and others. Yet the widespread but sporadic outbursts in the countryside at the time of the revolution of 1905 took even the Socialist Revolutionaries by surprise.

Thus, shortly before the outbreak of the First World War, the Russian peasants were still largely unpredictable, though no longer unknown, to many Russian politicians and intellectuals. There was still a considerable communication problem between the literate world and the largely illiterate world of the village commune. Russian terminology vividly reflects differences between these worlds: the community of society as a whole (*obshchestvo*) is distinguished from the small commonwealth of the commune (*obshchina*). Society had congresses (*s"ezdy*), the commune had gatherings (*skhody*); the former term implies that the meetings were reached on horseback or by vehicle, the latter that they were reached on foot. The riding lord and the walking peasant symbolise both institutional and social differences, different outlooks and emotional responses. The literate world's view of the peasant was as liable to be distorted as the peasant's view of the wider society.

When the Bolsheviks overthrew the Provisional Government and seized power, in November 1917, they immediately passed two decrees, the first on peace, the second on land. The hastily fudged-up decree on land abolished private ownership of estates and foresaw a settlement of the land question by the Constituent Assembly. The programme envisaged that the nationalised land would be available to anyone willing to work it without hired labour; the amount allotted to each family would be determined according to the number of either hands (workers) or mouths (consumers). Lenin, in fact, had in large part taken over the agrarian programme of the Socialist Revolutionaries he regarded as his political opponents. It was in this way that he secured the acquiescence, if not the support, of the overwhelming majority of the Russian people in 1917.

The land question was, thus, on the agenda from the start of Bolshevik

The Russian material in this volume has been translated by T. M. Myskow and R. E. F. Smith.

rule. It inevitably involved some consideration of the peasants. Russian politicians of the time were often men with professional training, or intellectuals; sometimes they had cosmopolitan experience and sympathies, or they saw Russia's future as being forged in the main by the industrial working class. Most Russian politicians were urbanites in a backward agrarian land; to them the peasant was largely a regrettable relict of the past, the visible sign of Russia's backwardness, to be outlived or abolished as soon as possible. There was much sympathy for, but little firmly-based understanding of the life of, the majority of Russians; disdain for and a rejection of the 'dark people' of the countryside seem to have been both characteristic of urban intellectuals, and the politically dominant attitude.

Views of, and attitudes to, the peasants differed widely among politicians and intellectuals in the period after the First World War. Among the Bolsheviks, this was partly because of the continuing gap between Soviet power in the towns and the life in the countryside, where Soviet authority was not effectively established until the late 1920s. The two short works by Gorky and Chayanov translated here, and originally published within a few years of the establishment of Bolshevik rule in Russia, illustrate how widely divergent such views were around 1920; the extracts from Bol'shakov's work serve to show something of the peasant reality of the time.

The first item, by the writer Maxim Gorky, is called *On the Russian Peasantry*. Its publishing history is somewhat curious. In October 1921 Gorky left Russia for Finland and then travelled with Zinovii Grzhebin to Berlin [*Letopis', vyp. 3, 1959: 252-3*]. Grzhebin, together with Aleksandr Tikhonov (who wrote under the pseudonyms A. and N. Serebrov) and I. P. Ladyzhnikov, had in 1918 organised the World Literature Publishing House (*Vsemirnaya literatura*) with the agreement of the People's Commissariat of Enlightenment. In December 1921 Grzhebin wrote to Gorky about his negotiations with *Nieuwe Rotterdamsche Courant* about printing *On the Russian Peasantry*, and enquired when Gorky intended to finish the first article and to write the others [*Letopis', vyp. 3, 1959: 258*]. Almost a fortnight later, Gorky wrote to Ladyzhnikov saying that he was trying to write an article on the Russian peasantry, but that it was '. . . not going easily, I don't feel like writing and the writing is dismal' [*Letopis', vyp. 3, 1959: 261*]. On 8 January 1922, however, he informed Ladyzhnikov that he had finished the article, and sent him the manuscript a week or so later [*Letopis', vyp. 3, 1959: 266, 267*]. The Danish journal *Politiken* published four items by Gorky [*April 2, 4, 6 and 9*], with an introduction stressing Gorky's importance as the voice of Russia in exile, and claiming that the article was to be published in the world's leading journals. (I am most grateful to Bjarne Nørretranders for finding these articles.) The four sections of this version of what became *On the Russian Peasantry* were entitled: Anarchy; Cruelty; Scepticism, and The Future. They were published in French in September 1922, the month Ladyzhnikov published Gorky's revised version in Berlin [*Gorki, 1922: 533-6, 576-9 and 613-8*]. They also appeared in the Milan journal *Il Secolo* in 1922 [*April 2,*

4, 6 and 9]. (I am most grateful to K. W. Humphreys and Aldo Giungi for finding these articles.) The first of the four sections had also appeared in Russian early in 1922, published in *Rupor* [*1922, No. 1: 4-5*], a Russian émigré journal in Bulgaria; another émigré journal, *Novaya Rossiya*, also published the item [*No. 2: 141-144*]. Meanwhile, Gorky had been attacked in the Soviet press as a neo-westerniser [*Izvestiya, No. 93, 28 April 1922: 3*] on the basis of the Danish publication; the article was signed 'ERDE' (Russian for the initials RD; the author has not so far been identified). Surely, it was claimed, Gorky realised the harm he would do worker-peasant Russia 'by these inauspicious pamphleteering novellas which will, of course, be seized on with keen delight by the entire bourgeois press?' There was also a mocking poem by Dem'yan Bednyi [*Pravda, No. 160, 20 July 1922*].

The Ladyzhnikov version of *On the Russian Peasantry*, from which the present translation has been made, differs in many minor respects from the part of the text published in Danish, Russian and French. A few excerpts from it have appeared in English [*Shanin, 1971: 369-71*]. A French version, authorised by Gorky, appeared in 1925 [*Gorki, 1925: 101-187*]. The item has not been included in Gorky's works published in the U.S.S.R. Svetlana Alliluyeva [*1969: 159*], Stalin's daughter, states that it was censored from a literary chronicle of the 1920s she and other researchers prepared in 1957-8; it was thrown out because 'it wasn't permissible to "vilify the icon"'. It thus shares the fate of Gorky's articles against Lenin [see *Gorky, 1968*].

The second item included here consists of chapters taken from *The Soviet Countryside*, a short book (143 pages and almost 30 additional pages of statistical materials) which focuses on what Bol'shakov observed in one small area of Tver' *guberniya* during 1917-24. Goritsy *volost'* was a typical *volost'* of the *guberniya*, remote from the communications network: the Volga was 40 *verstas*, the nearest railway stations 45 and 75 *verstas* distant. 'Apart from agriculture supported by the off-farm crafts and trades usual in the central *guberniyas*, there was no way here of making a living' [*Bol'shakov, 1924a: 13*].

The *volost'* had an area of 43,288 *desyatinas*, but more than a tenth of this was taken up by lakes, and as much as one third by almost impenetrable peat bogs covered with cranberry bushes; total useful land amounted to 23,767 *desyatinas*. The soils in the area are clay podzols, muddy, thin and unproductive. In 1920 the total population was 9,676 (including 4,182 able-bodied persons of both sexes), and there were 74 settlements with an average population of 130 persons in 15-20 households in each hamlet. In general terms, as the table shows, the *volost'* was close to the average for Tver' *guberniya* in a number of respects, though evidently somewhat wilder than average in terms of physical environment.

Bol'shakov (1887- ?) was a local man who lived in the area he was describing throughout the period involved. He stressed this himself: 'I was observing Goritsy *volost'* throughout the whole period with which I deal. I am well acquainted with all the economic conditions and the daily life of the

	Tver' guberniya	Goritsy volost'
Available land of which	100%	100%
Arable land, gardens	20·1%	27·8%
Meadows, scrub	34·3%	22·1%
Pasture	15·5%	4·0%
Forest	30·1%	46·1%
Livestock per 100 persons	44	44
Farms without livestock	15·7%	15·7%
Farms without cows	19·9%	18·7%

volost' since I am myself a peasant from there and have my peasant farm in the *volost'* [*1924a: 15*]. This statement, however, should not be taken to mean that Bol'shakov was by any means an average peasant. He was also a historian of Russia, as well as of his locality; in 1924, the year in which *The Soviet Countryside* appeared, his book *Auxiliary Historical Disciplines* was published in its fourth edition. A year later, together with the professional historian N. A. Rozhkov, he produced a three-part collection of materials on Russian history [*Bol'shakov, Rozhkov, 1925*]; this was reissued, with an amended title, within a year [*Bol'shakov, Rozhkov, 1925-6*]. A later work on the countryside from 1917 to 1927 [*Bol'shakov, 1927*] had a preface by M. I. Kalinin, president of the Russian Central Executive Committee, and S. F. Ol'denburg, an Orientalist who was secretary of the Academy of Sciences, 1904-29.

No doubt it was Bol'shakov's standing as a historian which gained him some official support and helped him to check official statistical data against what he saw and heard, and against information supplied by local peasants and others who knew and accepted him; it also meant he had access to a range of local official materials available to few. He was able, for instance, to use the archives of the local Soviet insurance office and of the local hospital, and the account and receipt books of the Volost' Executive Committee and other similar materials. He verified prices by his own observations and by talking to local traders who knew the market. Many of these written materials were lost in the turbulent years of the civil war, partly owing to the normal hazards of inefficiency, partly as a result of early Soviet administrative reorganisation; and partly for the simple reason that there was such a severe shortage of paper that the blank backs of documents were used for writing other documents; when the paper had been used on both sides it was then used for wrapping. Bol'shakov [*1924a: 96*] mentions, for instance, that in 1921 he had been authorised to obtain some data relating to 1918 and 1919 from the Guberniya Food Commitee, but the documents had disappeared.

Bol'shakov realised the value of such materials. Indeed, he probably exaggerated their importance because of the vital significance for world history he attached to the revolutionary period through which he was living. Nevertheless, he was unable to avoid errors of presentation, calculation and argument which continued, characteristically, to bedevil many Russian works long after he was writing. As far as possible the translation given here incorporates footnote material into the text. Statistical tables have also been incorporated at relevant places in the text; but some statistical material, although it would be relevant and of interest, has been omitted because it is incomprehensible. It proved impossible to arrive at the figures Bol'shakov gives by the method he describes and on the basis of his data. A peculiar feature of *The Soviet Countryside* is that the section labelled 'Results' comes in the middle of the work. The book is not, in fact, a coherent unit, but includes a number of brief sketches, on various aspects of life in the area at the time, which follow the chapter on 'Results'.

Despite its flaws, this material, and the picture it gives, is specific and at times vivid in its down-to-earth detail. Bol'shakov's tendentious argument to show the declining burden of taxation on the peasants may be fantasy (at the very least, the problem needs more serious treatment than he gives it); his depiction of the countryside of his day, however, bears the stamp of authenticity. He sees, and is honest enough to report, not only the return to a largely in-kind economy in the aftermath of the First World War and the revolution, but also the weakness and ineffectiveness of Soviet power in the countryside. He points out some of the incomprehensible or stupid orders issued (not to tan sheepskins, for example), and the dodges and widespread illegal activities which often resulted, since people had to live somehow. He points out that the potato was the main food of the population, that 'Soviet tea' was just boiling water; he queries whether the peasant's lot had improved at that time, and tries to show the losses and the benefits resulting from the Bolshevik revolution. Above all, he shows how the Soviet system really worked, or failed to work, in one small area of European Russia about 1920, when the civil war was at its height. Thus, although he was ideologically committed to the Bolsheviks, his views of the world around him were not abstract conceptualisations derived from dogma, but were firmly realistic. Because of this, his material provides some background against which the items by Gorky and Chayanov may be seen, and which helps to assess their validity.

The Journey of my Brother Alexei to the Land of Peasant Utopia, is the first, and apparently the only extant, part of what is possibly the only Soviet peasant utopia [*Shaw, 1963: 279; this article, inaccurate in several details, touches mainly on literary aspects*]. It was written by A. V. Chayanov, under the pseudonym Ivan Kremnev, and published in 1920 by the State Publishing House in Moscow, but with a critical foreword by P. Orlovskii [*Masanov, Slovar' psevdonimov, II:78; based on Vladislavlev, 1924: 140*]. Orlovskii was a pseudonym of V. V. Vorovskii (1871-1923), a professional diplomat and publicist who wrote articles both on peasants and on the literary intelligentsia, including Gorky; Vorovskii also used the pseudonyms Y. Adamovich and M. Schwarz [*Lazić, 1973: 430*]. The utopia is a scarcely-veiled criticism of the narrow, somewhat joyless Bolshevik reality of 1920. The vehicle for this criticism is a story which starts in the then immediate future, the autumn of 1921, but mostly takes place in a de-urbanised Moscow of 1984.

To establish the utopian year of 1984, Chayanov has the hero see it in a newspaper. This fictional newspaper, *The Sign of the Zodiac* for Friday, 5

September 1984, was produced by Chayanov as a supplement to his story, and was included with the book. Unfortunately, most library copies of *The Journey* lack this interesting and curious item. The Lenin Library in Moscow was unable to supply it. It was only after considerable efforts over several years that a copy was found in another Soviet Library. A translation of this rare item is included on p. 110.

Gorky and Chayanov propounded widely different views of the Russian peasants, but both had to draw on their experiences of a common reality: Russia as it was developing in the first quarter of the twentieth century. The post-1917 emigration from Russia, and the trials and purges of the 1930s, largely eliminated the old intelligentsia and most of the former professional classes. The enormous growth of towns and industry created a vast demand for administrators and professionally trained personnel. The newcomers who filled these posts were often of peasant origin; it is widely held that this accounts for much of the crudity of Soviet day-to-day administration and of everyday life. The purges and the collectivisation of farms, with mass deportations of the richer peasants, who were labelled 'kulaks' as a term of political convenience rather than as a real category, certainly resulted in ferociously cruel treatment of millions of people; but whether such cruelty can be blamed on the town or the countryside is unclear. The crudity and cruelty of the Soviet period may well have been implicit in the longstanding structure of Russian society, with its lack of a sufficiently numerous middle class, and its despotic traditions. What is undoubted, however, is that, during the period of War Communism, 1918-1921, when Gorky was writing, the strict enforcement of cumpulsory appropriations and then the requisitioning of foodstuffs (*prodrazverstka*) from the countryside contributed greatly to a considerable decline in the sown area. The peasant not only had his produce seized by armed detachments of workers from the town, but any money he held declined in value because of inflation, while the prices of industrial commodities rose more rapidly than those of agricultural produce. To imagine in these circumstances that the peasant would look with favour on the the town seems to imply an even more romantic view of the saintlike peasant than the image of the simple muzhik Gorky was attacking.

Perhaps of greater interest is the view, reported by Gorky, that large factories 'only mean riots and all sorts of vice', that the relatively simple industries required by the countryside should be small and scattered. This view coincides with that of Chayanov.

In the practical aspects of peasant life, Chayanov drew from his experience of the mainly producer, not consumer, Russian co-operatives, and his work on the executive of the League for Agrarian Reform. This had been formed in April 1917, and included a wide spectrum of political opinion: Marxists, Socialist Revolutionaries, Populists, and at least one conservative.

Chayanov was an adherent of the practically-oriented Organisation and Production trend among agrarian reformers. These were mainly agricultural officers and teachers employed by zemstva in the late nineteenth and early twentieth centuries, when the numbers of such men increased rapidly. By the time of the 1905 revolution, a well-argued case for the advantages of small-scale production in agriculture had been made; later, Chayanov summed up and developed the argument put forward at that time that the concepts of classical economics, derived from capitalist economies, were inapplicable when analysing Russian peasant economy. Chayanov, then, in common with this school of thought, regarded the Marxist analysis of the agrarian problem as mistaken, and the Social Democrat and Social Revolutionary answer of land reform by socialisation (Bol'shakov's 'nationalisation') as inadequate in practical terms. A change in ownership would not automatically resolve the practical difficulties of farming.

The solutions to the agrarian problem propounded by the Organisation and Production school were concerned largely with practical measures which could in great part be carried through without changing the political system. The field experience and research of the adherents of this trend of thought led not only to the design of new methods of carrying out budget surveys and analysis of weakly-monetised peasant farms, but also went far towards outlining a theory of peasant economy as a system comparable with socio-economic formations in the Marxist sense [*see Chayanov, 1967: 1-28*]. Chayanov's utopia is a depiction of such a system in operation. It is, thus, not a mere personal fantasy, but an imagined realisation of the concept of peasant socialism.

In a broad sense, then, Chayanov's 1984 is at least as firmly rooted in reality as Gorky's account of contemporary peasant society. This is scarcely surprising, in view of Chayanov's career. Six years after his appointment in 1913 to the Petrovsko-Razumovskii Agricultural Institute (now the Timiryazev Agricultural Academy) he took charge of its economics section (later the Institute of Agricultural Economy) of which he was Director until his arrest in 1930. Chayanov's pluralistic views and liberal attitude to the making of the Russian revolution had not endeared him to the Bolsheviks, especially at the time of mass collectivisation. Kremnev's mention of the triumph of the peasant parties in the 1930s was probably remembered during Chayanov's trial. Solzhenitsyn [*1974: 50*] mentions that Chayanov was arrested again in 1948; but Chayanov's widow gives his date of death at 30 March 1939. Chertkov [*8: 448*] states that he died in 1939 at Alma-Ata. Chayanov had not only held a central position in the field of agricultural economics and produced important works dealing with many aspects of peasant farming; he also wrote and published some verse and stories, a play and a couple of booklets on art.

The concerns of Gorky and of Chayanov remain with us today. The problem of violence and cruelty is not a monopoly either of peasants or of the U.S.S.R.; the tyranny of state power and the organisation of society, the role of towns, the level of industrial development and the nature of work and leisure are problems throughout the world today. The utopia Chayanov depicted is in many ways the positive image of Gorky's negative picture. Gorky asserted that the peasant did not justly evaluate the town as 'the inextinguishable hearth of a demanding and ever-exploring thought, the source of stimulating events and phenomena'. Chayanov sided with the peasant critics who saw little or no return by the town for the food and labour taken from the village. Gorky stressed the contribution of the urban worker and quoted, with evident disbelief, perhaps even disapproval, a peasant who said: 'Workers are greedy, they want everything they see, but the muzhik is satisfied with little'. In Chayanov's Moscow of 1984 the greedy worker is controlled by reducing the size of towns, by changing their functions and by the state regulating industry by the very down-to-earth (and up-to-date) means of control of fuel. But Chayanov's view is not one of mere negative primitivism. His breadth of outlook and the range of his interests mean that his little story includes comments on such matters as art, eating and love—and these passages, though they may sometimes seem odd to us, are not extraneous embellishments, but are an attempt to show something of the whole man in utopia.

The two works, then, are more than the intrinsically interesting, but curious, oddities of the Soviet 1920s they seem to be. They help us to see the range of views held at that time by Russian intellectuals about the peasant world in which they lived.

Bol'shakov adds a third element. His description of conditions in one limited area at this nadir in Russia's history helps to offset the views of these two very different representatives of the Russian intelligentsia by showing what conditions were really like at the time. The poverty and deprivation he depicts were not by any means limited to the area described which, after all, was in north-central European Russia, not a completely remote backwoods area. Yet it was this impoverished rural world which was the basis both for Gorky's vitriol and for Chayanov's vision of Arcady. In a decade this world was to be irredeemably changed by industrialisation and collectivisation. Neither Gorky nor Chayanov gives us a scholarly analysis of Russian peasant society and its future; both display considerable prejudice. Half a century later, Gorky's belief in progress based on urban industry appears simplistic and grossly over-optimistic, while Chayanov's faith in the social values of a simpler society may arouse sympathy, but appears still to be a utopian dream.

Notes appear at the end of the particular item. Original author's notes are indicated by asterisks; translators' notes are numbered.

Note on the Sources of George Orwell's 1984

R. E. F. Smith

George Orwell's well-known anti-utopian novel, *1984*, firmly established this date as a symbol in the English language. Orwell's novel, first published in 1949, was influenced by Evgenii Zamyatin, whose own anti-utopian novel *We* (in Russian *My*) he knew via a French translation [*Shane, 1968: 140*]. Orwell's choice of the seemingly arbitrary date of 1984 for his anti-utopia has been speculatively accounted for by Gleb Struve as 'a joke on his readers by merely reversing the last two figures' of the year when he was writing [*Struve, 1972: 50. Cf. Bondarenko, Grani, no. 56, 1964: 198*]. Struve had told Orwell about Zamyatin in the early 1940s, and had lent him the French version of *We*. Deutscher [*1955: 36*] claimed that 'Orwell borrowed the idea of *1984*, the plot, the chief characters, the symbols and the whole climate of his story' from Zamyatin. Did he borrow the date from him too?

Gleb Struve considers this link most unlikely. 'Zamyatin *may* have known Chayanov. This does not, however, imply that he knew his Utopian novel (or *povest'*). There is certainly no mention of it, or of 1984, in anything which Zamyatin left behind. There is no such date in his own *We*. But even if he knew Chayanov's story and the date in it, how could he have passed on that knowledge to Orwell? Orwell knew nothing about Zamyatin and his *We* before 1944 (see his letter to me of February 17, 1944).

'I am still inclined to hold on to my "speculative" explanation of Orwell's date. It is true that he began writing it much earlier, but by 1947 he knew that the date of publication would be *1948*. As for Chayanov's date, which may appear quite arbitrary, its explanation, I think, must be the following: Chayanov situates the overthrow of the Bolshevik regime (its replacement by the peasant Soviets) in 1934; 1984 would thus mark the *fiftieth* anniversary of the peasant rule, something to remember and to stress. The identity of the dates in Chayanov and in Orwell is a pure coincidence.' [*Private communication of 14 February 1976; also Struve, 1976*].

That 1984 is, in fact, the fiftieth anniversary of a crucial date is not quite clear. In his Utopia, Chayanov states that there had been a permanent peasant majority on the Central Executive Committee and at congresses from 1932; the year 1934 had seen a rising, the first purely peasant-class Council of People's Commissars and the decree on the destruction of towns. These events of 1934 were certainly important for his tale, but Chayanov himself does not stress 1934 as a crucial date, nor does he make any reference to a celebration of this anniversary. Indeed, he is sufficiently careless of this date to have Nikifor Minin in the story refer to the decree on the destruction of towns as being forty, not fifty, years old (p. 78 below). He seems to attach greater importance to the fact that 'Varvarin's rising of 1937 was the last manifestation of the political role of the towns' (p. 87 below). It might be supposed that, in terms of his story, the suppression of this rising would be a more important occasion to celebrate.

If the date 1984 were a mere coincidence, it would be a strange one. In fact, however, a more satisfactory source for the date 1984 is to be found elsewhere. Matthew Hodgart [*Gross, 1971: 140*] has called attention to the probability that the date 1984 is taken from Jack London's *The Iron Heel*, first published in 1907. This work was well known to Orwell, who praised its content, and it would also have been accessible to Chayanov, since a Russian translation of London's complete works reached its second edition before the First World War. This, then, is almost certainly the origin of the date both for Chayanov and for Orwell. There appears to be no obvious reason for the choice of this date, which occurs in chapter XXI of *The Iron Heel*, but is only one of a dozen dates in the future in London's novel.

What is curious, therefore, is that both Chayanov and Orwell should have chosen to date their stories 1984. Perhaps Orwell did not choose the date quite independently of Chayanov. Under the pseudonym *Botanik X* (i.e. 'X' the botanist), Chayanov published a story in 1918 called *The Hairdresser's Doll, or the last love of M., the Moscow architect* [*1918*]. This contained some features which link it with the Utopia (the panopticum with its wax effigies, for example); it was dedicated to E. T. A. Hoffman, the German writer whose heroes gave their name to the Serapion Brothers, an early Soviet group of writers whose mentor Zamyatin was [*Oulanoff, 1966: 17*]. Zamyatin also had been associated with the *Zavety* group. *Zavety* (Behests) was a literary and political journal of Socialist Revolutionary tendency which first appeared in 1912. It was at this period that Chayanov was making his mark in agricultural and co-operative circles. Zamyatin, therefore, may have known of Chayanov from as early as 1912. *We* itself was written in 1920-21 at the very time when Chayanov's Utopia appeared. Zamyatin knew English and had worked in England in 1916-17. Although it is unlikely that he can have been instrumental in suggesting the date 1984 to Orwell, he remains a possible link between the milieu in which the Russian 1984 emerged and the English-speaking world.

Chayanov himself, however, appears to have been in England in 1922. Again under the pseudonym *Botanik X* he published *The Venetian Mirror, or the wondrous adventures of the glass man* [*1923*]; this, too, has passages reminiscent of the Utopia and bears the subscription at the end of the text 'London, 1922'. It is no more than speculation, but it is not totally inconceivable that Chayanov spoke of his 1984 Utopia to English friends and that this date survived in oral tradition for twenty-five years to remind Orwell of a date he had read, but perhaps not consciously noted, in *The Iron Heel*. Even if this were so, the mystery, of course, remains: why did Chayanov chose the date 1984?

On the Russian Peasantry

by

Maxim Gorky

1922

THE I.P. LADYZHNIKOV PUBLISHING HOUSE, BERLIN

I HAVE been asked by people I am accustomed to take seriously what I think about Russia. All my thoughts about my country—more precisely, about the Russian people and about the majority of them, the peasantry—weigh very heavily on me. It would be easier not to answer the question, but I have seen and know too much to have the right to be silent. Yet I beg you to understand that I condemn no one, justify no one, I am simply recording the forms resulting from the mass of my impressions. An opinion is not a condemnation, and if my opinions turn out to be mistaken, it will not offend me.

*   *   *

Any people is essentially an anarchic element; the people want to eat as much as possible and work as little as possible, they want to have all rights and no obligations. The atmosphere of lack of rights in which the people have been accustomed to live since ancient times has convinced them of the legality of a lack of rights, of the zoological naturalness of anarchism. This is particularly applicable to the mass of the Russian peasantry, who have experienced slavery in a cruder form and longer than the other peoples of Europe. For hundreds of years the Russian peasant has dreamt of a state with no right to influence the will of the individual, his freedom of action, of a state without power over man. In the unrealisable hope of attaining the equality of all with unlimited freedom for each, the Russian people have attempted to create such a state in Cossackdom, the Zaporozh'e Seche. In the darkness of the Russian sectarian's soul, the concept of a fabulous 'Kingdom of Opona' lives to this day; it exists somewhere 'on the edge of the earth', there people live in tranquillity, ignorant of 'the vanities of anti-Christ', and of the town afflicted by the convulsive torment of creating culture. The instinct of the nomad seems to survive in the Russian peasant, he regards the labour of the tiller of the soil as a curse of God, and is sick with 'the desire for new places'. He almost lacks the fighting desire to establish himself on a chosen spot and influence his surroundings in his own interests, or at any rate has it very weakly developed; and, if he does decide to do this, a laborious and fruitless struggle awaits him. The village greets with distrust and hostility those who attempt to introduce into its life something of themselves, something new, and it rapidly expels and rejects them from its midst. But more frequently it is the innovators who clash with the unconquerable conservatism of the village and themselves decide to leave. There is always somewhere to go; the empty plain unrolls on every side and the distance calls seductively.

The talented Russian historian, Kostomarov, says: 'There was opposition to the state among the people; owing to the excessive geographical space, however, it was expressed in flight and the shunning of obligations which the state imposed on the people, but not by effective opposition and not by struggle'. Since those times the population of the Russian plain has increased, the 'geographical space' has become restricted, but the psychology remains and is epitomised in the curious proverb which advises 'don't run away from anything, but don't do anything'.

From early childhood, as soon as he can get up on his hindlegs, Western man sees everywhere around him the monumental results of his ancestors' labour. From the canals of Holland to the tunnels of the Italian riviera and the vineyards of Vesuvius, from the great works of England to the mighty Silesian factories, the whole of Europe is closely covered by the grandiose incarnations of the organised will of the people, a will which set itself a proud aim: to subordinate the elemental forces of nature to the rational interests of man. The land is in the hands of man and man is its real ruler. The child of the West absorbs this impression, and it makes him aware of the worth of man, gives him a respect for his labour and a feeling for his personal significance, as the heir of the marvels of his ancestor's labour and creativity.

Such thoughts, such feelings and values cannot arise in the heart of the Russian peasant. The boundless, flat country, in which straw-thatched, wooden hamlets closely huddle together, has a poisonous quality which devastates a man, and empties him of desire. When a peasant goes beyond the limits of his hamlet and looks at the emptiness around him, after a time he feels that this emptiness has filled his heart. Nowhere around are these stable traces of labour and creative work to be seen. The seats of the landlords? But they are few and occupied by enemies. The towns? But they are distant and are little more significant culturally than the hamlet. Around is a limitless plain, in its centre an insignificant little man, cast up on this boring earth for hard labour. Man is overcome by indifference, which kills his ablity to think, to remember what he has seen, to generate his own ideas from his experience. A historian of Russian culture described the peasantry as: 'a multitude of superstitions and no ideas'.

This sad judgment is confirmed by the whole of Russian folklore.

*   *   *

No doubt 'the vital gold of luxuriant cornfields' is fine in summer, but in autumn the ragged, bare earth lies before the tiller once again, and again demands yet more hard labour. Then a severe six-month winter sets in, the land is covered in a blinding white shroud, the snowstorms howl fiercely and man gasps from idleness and boredom in his close, dirty hut. Of all that he does there remains on earth only straw and the straw-thatched hut—and fires destroy that three times in the life of each generation.

The technically primitive labour of the countryside is unbelievably heavy; the peasants call it 'suffering' (*strada*), from the verb 'to suffer'. The burden of labour, in conjunction with its insignificant results, intensifies the instinct of property in the peasant, making him almost immune to the influence of those teachings which explain all man's sins in terms of the power of this instinct.

The townsman's labour is varied, stable and enduring. From amorphous lumps of lifeless ore he creates machines and apparatus of astounding complexity, animated by his reason, alive. He has subordinated the forces of nature to his high aims, and they serve him like the jinns of the Eastern fables served King Solomon. He has created around him an atmosphere of reason, 'a second natural environment'; everywhere he sees his energy embodied in various mechanisms and objects, in thousands of books and paintings; and everywhere there are the imprints of the majestic torments of his spirit, his dreams and his hopes; of his love and hatred, his doubts and of his beliefs, in which a desire for new forms, ideas, deeds and a tormenting struggle to discover the secrets of nature and to find the meaning of existence, burns inextinguishably.

Enslaved by the power of the state, he remains internally free, and it is by the power of this freedom of spirit that he destroys obsolete forms of life and creates new ones. A man of deeds, he has created for himself a life tormentingly tense, vicious, but fine in its fullness. He is the originator of all social ills, the perversions of the flesh and of the spirit, author of lies and social hyprocrisy, but he has also created a microscope of self-criticism which allows him to see with terrible clarity all his faults and crimes, all his voluntary and involuntary mistakes, the slightest movements of his ever-dissatisfied spirit.

A great sinner before his neighbours and perhaps a still greater one before himself, he is a great martyr to his strivings which, distorting and destroying him, give birth to all new things, both new torments and joys of existence. Like the accursed Ahasuerus, his spirit passes into the limitless future, somewhere in the heart of the cosmos or in the cold emptiness of the universe which perhaps he will fill with the emanation of his phychic and physical energy, creating in time something unattainable with the concepts of our present-day intellect.

Only the utilitarian results of the development of spiritual culture are important to the instinct, only what improves the external and material conditions of life, even though it should be a glaring and humiliating lie.

To the intellect the process of creation is important in itself; the intellect is stupid, like the sun, it works for no gain.

*   *   *

There lived in Russia a certain Ivan Bolotnikov, a man of singular fate: as a child he was taken prisoner by the Tatars during one of their attacks on the border towns of the Moscow state; as a youth he was sold into slavery to the Turks and he worked on the Turkish galleys; Venetians bought him out of slavery and, after living for a time in the aristocratic republic of the Doges, he returned to Russia.

This was in 1606. The Moscow boyars had just poisoned the talented Tsar, Boris Godunov, and killed that clever daredevil, the enigmatic youth who, taking the name of Dmitri, son of Ivan the Terrible, occupied the Moscow throne and, striving to overcome the Asiatic morals of the Muscovites, said to their faces: 'You consider yourselves the most righteous people on earth, but you are debauched and malicious; you have little love for your neighbours and are not disposed to do good'.

He was killed, and the cunning, two-faced prince Vasilii Shuiskii was chosen as Tsar; a second Pretender appeared, also giving himself out as the son of Ivan the Terrible, and then there began in Russia the bloody tragedy of political dissolution known in history as the Time of Troubles. Ivan Bolotnikov attached himself to the second Pretender; he was put in command of a small detachment of the Pretender's supporters and went with them to Moscow, urging the villeins and peasants: 'Beat the boyars, take their wives and all their property. Beat the traders and rich people, divide their property between you.'

This enticing programme of primitive communism attracted to Bolotnikov tens of thousands of villeins, peasants and vagabonds; more than once they defeated Tsar Vasilii's troops, though the latter were better armed and organised; they besieged Moscow and were repulsed with great difficulty by the forces of the boyars and trading people. Finally, this first powerful mutiny of peasants was quenched in a bloodbath, Bolotnikov was captured, his eyes were gouged out and he was drowned.

Bolotnikov's name has not been preserved in peasant memory; his life and activity left no heritage of songs or legends. And, in general Russian peasant oral tradition has nothing to say on the decade 1602–13, the bloody Time of Troubles, which a historian has called 'a school of insubordination, lack of leadership, political folly, duplicity, deceit, frivolity and petty egoism incapable of assessing the common needs'. But all this left no trace either on the Russian peasant's daily life or in his memory.

The memory of Fra Dolcino has been preserved in the legends of Italy, the Czechs remember Jan Žižka, the peasants of Germany also remember Thomas Münzer and Florian Heier, the French the heroes and martyrs of the Jacquerie and the English Watt Tyler; the people have retained songs, legends and tales of all these. The Russian peasant does not know his heroes and leaders, the fanatics of love, justice and vengeance.

Fifty years after Bolotnikov, the Don Cossack, Stepan Razin, raised the peasantry in almost the whole Volga area and moved with them on Moscow, stirred by the same idea of political and economic equality. For almost three years his bands plundered and slaughtered the boyars and merchants; he won regular battles with the forces of Tsar Alexei Romanov, his mutiny threatened to raise the whole of rural Rus'. He was defeated and then quartered. The popular memory retains two or three songs about him, but their purely popular origin is doubtful and their meaning was incomprehensible to the peasants even at the beginning of the nineteenth century.

No less powerful and extensive in scope was the mutiny made under Catherine the Great by the Ural Cossack, Pugachev; 'the Cossacks' last attempt to fight the state regime', as the historian S. F. Platonov defined this mutiny. The peasants have kept no bright memories of Pugachev or of any of all the other less significant political achievements of the Russian people.

Exactly the same can be said of them as was said by the historian of the terrible Time of Troubles: 'All these risings changed nothing, they introduced nothing new into the mechanism of the state, into the system of concepts, into morals and aspirations . . .'

The verdict is aptly complemented by the conclusion of a foreigner who carefully observed the Russian people. 'This people has no historical memory. It does not know its past—and seems even not to want to know it'. The Grand Prince Sergei Romanov told me that in 1913, when the tercentenary of the Romanov dynasty was being celebrated, and Tsar Nicholas was in Kostroma, Nikolai Mikhailovich, also a Grand Prince and a gifted author of a whole series of solid historical works, said to the Tsar, pointing to a crowd of many thousands of peasants: 'No, they are just as they were in the seventeenth century when they chose Michael as Tsar, just the same; this is bad, what do you think?'

The Tsar kept silent. They say he was always silent when asked serious questions. This is a kind of wisdom, if it is not a cunning ploy or caused by fear.

*   *   *

Cruelty is what has amazed and tormented me all my life. Where and in what lie the roots of human cruelty? I have thought a good deal about this, and have not understood and still do not.

Once, long ago, I read a book with the ominous title 'Progress as the Evolution of Cruelty'.

By skilfully selecting his facts, the author proved that, with progress, men torment one another with more and more voluptuousness, both physically and spiritually. I read this book with anger and disbelief, and soon forgot its paradoxes.

But now, after the terrible madness of the European war and the bloody events of the revolution—now I remember these mordant paradoxes ever more frequently. But I would note that Russian cruelty does not seem to evolve, its forms do not apparently change.

An early seventeenth-century chronicler recounts how people were tormented in his day; 'they put gunpowder in their mouths and set fire to it, others they stuffed with gunpowder from below, they cut through women's breasts and, threading ropes through the wounds, hung them on these ropes'.

In the eighteenth and nineteenth centuries they did the same on the Don and on the Ural: stuffing a stick of dynamite into a man from below, they blew him up.

I think that a feeling af particular cruelty, cold-blooded and, as it were, testing the limits of human endurance of pain, as it were, studying the tenacity and endurance of life, is exclusively peculiar to the Russian people —just as exclusively as the sense of humour is to the Englishman.

One feels in Russian cruelty a diabolical refinement, there is something precise and deliberate about it. This characteristic can scarcely be explained by the terms psychosis, sadism, words which essentially explain nothing in general. The heritage of alcoholism? I do not think the Russian people was more poisoned by alcohol than any other people of Europe although it is conceivable, given the poor diet of the Russian peasants, that the poison of alcohol acts on the psyche more powerfully in Russia than in other countries where the people's diet is more abundant and varied.

We may conceive that reading the lives of saints and great martyrs— the favourite reading of the literate in remote villages—influenced the development of this inventive cruelty.

If the instances of cruelty were the expression of the perverted psychology of individuals there would be no need to speak of them; in this event they would be material for the psychiatrist and not the writer dealing with everyday life. But I have in mind only the collective amusements in tormenting man.

The peasants in Siberia dug pits and lowered Red Army prisoners into them upside down, leaving their legs to the knees above ground; then they gradually filled in the pit with soil, watching by the convulsions of the legs which of the victims was more resistant, livelier, and which would be the last to die.

The Trans-Baikal Cossacks trained their young men in the use of the sabre on prisoners.

In Tambov Guberniya Communists were nailed with railway spikes by their left hand and left foot to trees a metre above the soil, and they watched the torments of these deliberately oddly-crucified people.

They would open a prisoner's belly, take out the small intestine and nailing it to a tree or telegraph pole they drove the man around the tree with blows, watching the intestine unwind through the wound. Stripping a captured officer naked, they tore strips of skin from his shoulders in the form of shoulder straps, and knocked in nails in place of pips; they would pull off the skin along the lines of the sword belt and trouser stripes— this operation was called 'to dress in uniform'. It, no doubt, demanded much time and considerable skill.

Many similar horrors were perpetrated, but revulsion prevents me from adding to the number of descriptions of these bloody amusements. Who was crueller, Whites or Reds? Probably they were equal; after all, both of them were Russians. In any event, history gives a very clear answer to the question of degrees of cruelty: he who is the most active is the most cruel . . .

*   *   *

I think that women are nowhere beaten as mercilessly and terribly as in the Russian village; and probably in no other country do proverbs offer such advice. 'Hit your wife with the butt of the axe, get down and see whether she is breathing. If she is and shamming, she wants more'. 'A wife is nice twice; when she is brought into the house and when she is carried to the grave'. 'There is no court for old women and cattle'. 'The more you beat the old woman, the tastier the soup will be'.

Hundreds of such aphorisms, embodying the people's wisdom accumulated over centuries, circulate in the countryside; they listen to this advice, their children are brought up on it.

Children, too, are assiduously beaten. When I wanted to learn about the nature of criminal offences in the Moscow district, I looked through the 'Reports of the Moscow Palace of Justice' for ten years, 1901–10, and was depressed by the number of cases of child torture as well as other crimes against minors. In general, in Russia they very much like beating people up; it does not matter whom. 'Popular wisdom' puts a high price on a beaten man: 'For a man that has been beaten you have to offer two unbeaten ones, but even then you may not clinch the bargain'.

There are even sayings which consider fights as an essential condition for a full life. 'Oh, it's a jolly life, only there's no-one to beat'.

I have asked those who were active in the civil war whether they were at all uneasy in killing one another. No, they were not.

'He has a weapon, I have a weapon, so we are equal; what's the odds, if we kill one another there'll be more room in the land'.

Once I had an extremely original reply to this question from a soldier of the European War, now commander of a considerable detachment of the Red Army.

'An internal war, that's nothing! But internecine strife against others, that sticks in the gullet. I'll tell you straight, comrade, it's easier to kill a Russian. Our people are many, our economy is poor; well, if a hamlet is burnt, what's the loss. It would have burnt down itself in due course. And anyway, it's our own internal affair, a sort of manoeuvres, for learning, you might say. But when I happened to be in Prussia early in the other war—my God, I was so sorry for the people there, their villages, the towns and the whole set-up! What a splendid economy we destroyed for no known cause. It made you sick! . . . When I was wounded I was almost glad, it was so hard to look at the ugliness of life. Then I was in the Caucasus against Yudenich, there there were Turks and other darkies. Very poor people, good chaps, smiling, you know, but nobody knows why. You beat him, and he smiles. I was sorry for them, too, I mean, each of them has his job, they're attached to life in their own way . . .'.

This was said by a man, humane in his own fashion, on good terms with his soldiers and evidently respected and even loved by them, who loves his military profession.

I tried to tell him something about Russia, about her significance in the world; he listened thoughtfully, pulling at his cigarette, then with a weary look he sighed and said: 'Yes, of course, ours was a special state, quite an extraordinary one; but now, I feel it's finally sunk in villainy!'

It seems to me that the war has produced many people like him, and that the leaders of the countless and senseless bands are of this mental cast.

*   *   *

In discussing cruelty, one can hardly ignore the nature of the Jewish pogroms in Russia. The fact that these were permitted by the evil idiots who held power exonerates no-one and justifies nothing. In allowing the beating and pillaging of Jews, the idiots did not enjoin the terrorist hundreds taking part in the pogroms to cut off the breasts of Jewish women, beat their children, drive nails into Jewish skulls—all these bloody abominations must be seen as 'manifestations of the personal initiative of the masses'.

Well then, where, finally, is that kindly, contemplative Russian peasant, the indefatigable searcher after truth and justice, so convincingly and beautifully presented to the world by Russian nineteenth-century literature?

In my youth I earnestly sought for such a man throughout the Russian countryside, but did not find him. I met a harsh and cunning realist, well able to act the simpleton when it suited him. By nature he is no fool, and well he knows it. He has created a multitude of melancholy songs, coarse and cruel tales, and has made up thousands of proverbs embodying the experience of his hard life.

He knows that 'the muzhik is not stupid, but the commune is a fool', and that 'the commune is as strong as water, but as stupid as a pig'.

He says 'Don't fear devils, fear people'. 'Beat your own folk, others will fear you'.

He has no high regard for truth: 'Truth will not fill your belly'. 'What if it's a lie, so long as your belly is filled'. 'A just man does as much harm as a fool'.

Feeling himself up to any task, he says: 'Beat a Russian and he'll make you a watch'. And beat him you have to because 'Every day you're not too lazy to eat, but you're not too keen to work'.

He has thousands of similar such aphorisms: he knows how to use them skilfully, he hears them from childhood, and from childhood discovers how much bitter truth and sadness, how much self-mockery and resentment they hold. People, particularly townspeople, very much get in the way of his life, he considers them unnecessary on an earth literally manured with his sweat and blood, on an earth which he loves mystically; he unshakably knows and feels that by his flesh he is firmly alloyed to this soil that is his by blood-right and taken from him by robbery. Long before Lord Byron, he knew that 'The landlord's seat costs the peasant's sweat'. The literature of the folk-lover served the aims of political agitation and therefore idealised the muzhik; but by the end of the nineteenth century the attitude of literature to the countryside and to the peasant began to change decisively, becoming less compassionate and more candid. The new view of the peasants was initiated by Anton Chekhov with his stories 'In the Gulley' and 'The Muzhiks'.

The stories of the best of contemporary Russian writers, Ivan Bunin, appeared in the first years of the twentieth century.

His 'Night Conversation' and another story, 'The Hamlet', outstanding for the beauty of its language and its severe veracity, established a new critical attitude to the Russian peasantry. In Russia it is said of Bunin that, as a member of the gentry, he has a biased, even hostile, view of the muzhik. This is, of course, untrue; Bunin is simply a fine artist. But in Russian literature this century there is sharper and sadder evidence of the dreadful darkness of the countryside; there is 'Youth', a story written by the talented peasant from Orel *guberniya*, Ivan Volny; and there are the stories of the Moscow peasant, Semen Podyachev, as well as the stories by the Siberian peasant, Vsevolod Ivanov, a young writer of exceptional brilliance and power.

These people can scarcely be suspected of a prejudiced and hostile attitude to a milieu to which they are related by flesh and blood, and with which they have not yet broken their links. They, better than anyone else, know and understand peasant life, the countryside's sorrows and crude joys, the blindness of its reason and the harshness of its emotions.

To conclude this joyless sketch, I quote a story of a member of a scientific expedition which worked in the Urals in 1921. A peasant turned to the expedition with the following question: 'You are educated people, tell me then, what's to happen to me; a Bashkir killed my cow, so *of course,* I killed the Bashkir and then I took the cow away from his family, so tell me: shall I be punished for the cow?'

When they asked him whether he did not expect to be punished for the murder of the man, the muzhik answered calmly: 'That's nothing, people are cheap nowadays'.

The phrase 'of course' is here characteristic; it shows that murder has become a simple, usual matter. This is a result of the Civil War and of banditry.

Here is an example of how, sometimes, ideas new to the rural mind are perceived.

A rural teacher, the son of a peasant, wrote to me. 'Since the celebrated scientist, Darwin, has established scientifically the necessity for a merciless struggle for existence and has no objection to the destruction of weak and useless people, and since in olden times old people were taken off to die of hunger in ravines or set in trees and shaken down to their death, so, protesting against such harshness, I propose that useless people should be destroyed by more compassionate means. For example, poison them with something tasty, and so on. Such measures would alleviate the universal struggle for existence, i.e. its methods. We should deal similarly with weak-minded idiots, with madmen and congenital criminals, and perhaps also with the incurably sick, the hunch-backed, the blind and suchlike. Such legislation, of course, will not please our whining intelligentsia, but the time has come to stop paying attention to their conservative and counter-revolutionary ideology. Keeping useless people costs the nation too much and this item of expenditure should be reduced to nil'.

Many such and similar projects, letters and reports are now being written in Russia; they are very depressing, but also, despite their monstrosity, they make us feel that thought has been awakened in the countryside and, though clumsily, it is working in a direction completely new to it; the village is attempting to think of the state as a whole.

*   *   *

There is an opinion that the Russian peasant is somehow particularly deeply religious. I have never felt this, though. I think I have observed the spiritual life of the people carefully enough. I consider that a man who is illiterate and unaccustomed to think can be genuinely neither a theist nor an atheist, and that the path to a firm, deep faith leads through the desert of disbelief.

In talking with believing peasants and observing the life of various sects I was mainly struck by an organic, blind distrust of the questings of the intellect and of its work, I observed an attitude of mind which you should call the scepticism of ignorance.

In the efforts of the members of the sects to stand apart, to keep aloof from the state church organisation, I always felt a negative attitude not so much to ritual, and least of all to dogma, but to the system of state and urban life generally. In this rejection I could not perceive any original idea or signs of creative thought, any quest for new spiritual paths. It is simply a passive and sterile denial of phenomena and events, the relations and significance of which a weakly-developed intellect cannot comprehend.

I think the Revolution has quite definitely proved the fallacy of the belief that the peasantry in Russia is deeply religious. I do not consider the setting up of theatres and clubs in rural churches significant, although sometimes this was done, not because there was no other more convenient premises for a theatre, but with the clear aim of demonstrating free-thinking. There have also been more crudely blasphemous treatment of churches; it can be explained by hostility to 'the priests', by a desire to offend the cleric and at times by the naïvely daring curiosity of youth: 'What will happen to me if I insult what everyone venerates?'

There are other facts incomparably more important. The destruction of monasteries deeply revered by the people, the ancient Monastery of the Caves in Kiev and the Trinity Monastery of St. Sergius, which played an enormous historical and religious role, evoked among the peasantry neither protests nor disturbances, contrary to the confident expectations of certain politicians. It was as if these centres of religious life had suddenly lost the magic power which used to draw believers from all quarters of Russia's vast area. And yet, with weapons in their hands and with no concern for their lives, these peasants defended the hundreds of thousands of bushels of grain hidden from starving Moscow and Petersburg.

When provincial Soviets carried out post-mortems of 'imperishable' holy relics, deeply revered by the people, the latter observed these deeds with perfect calm, with a mute, dull curiosity. The examination of the relics was carried out with an extreme lack of tact, and often in a very crude manner, with the active participation of aliens, of people of other religious beliefs, with rough mockery of the feelings of those who believed in the sanctity and miraculous power of the relics. But that, too, aroused no protest from those who, only yesterday, had bowed before the tombs of the 'miracle-workers'. I have questioned several dozen eye-witnesses and participants of such exposure of ecclesiastic deceit: What had they felt when, instead of an imperishable and fragrant body, a crudely-made dummy or half-decayed bones were revealed before their eyes? Some said that a miracle had taken place; the holy bodies, knowing of the desecration intended by disbelievers, had left their tombs and hidden themselves. Others asserted that the deceit had been arranged by the monks only when they had learnt of the authority's intention to destroy the relics: 'They took out the real imperishable relics and replaced them with dummies'.

It is almost exclusively the old, illiterate country folk who talk thus. The younger and more literate peasants accept, of course, that there was deceit and say: 'It was right to do it, there is one deceit the less'. But then they have other thoughts, I reproduce them literally, as I wrote them down.

'Now that the monasteries' tricks have been shown up, we must quiz the doctors and various learned men, open their affairs to the people'. I had to press the man I was talking with for a long time before he would explain what he meant. Somewhat embarrassed he said: 'Of course, you don't believe this . . . but they say that now it's possible to poison the wind, and that would be the end of every living thing, man and beast. Now everyone is vicious, no-one has any pity'.

Another peasant, a member of an *uezd* Soviet, a self-declared Communist, developed this alarming thought still further. 'We need no miracles. We want to live in the clear light of day without anxiety, without terror. But miracles have been fixed in plenty. They've decided to bring electric light to the countryside; they say that there will be fewer fires. That's fine, God willing! Only let's hope they don't make any mistakes, turn some screw the wrong way and the whole village goes up in flames. You see how dangerous that is? And I'll say another thing; the townspeople are cunning, but the villages are stupid, they are easily fooled. And this is something big they've fixed on. The soldiers have been saying that in the War whole regiments were killed by electric light'.

I tried to dissipate Caliban's fears, and heard this sensible reply: 'There are some who know everything, and others know nothing; that's the root of all our trouble. How can I believe, if I know nothing?'

The complaints of the countryside on its dark ignorance are heard ever more frequently and sound ever more alarming. A Siberian, a lively young man who organised a partisan detachment in the rear of Kolchak's forces, said gloomily: 'Our people are not ready for events. They flounder about blindly. We smashed a detachment of Kolchak's men, took three machine-guns, a small gun, a small transport train, killed about fifty of them and ourselves lost seventy-one; there we were sitting, resting, when suddenly my lads asked me: don't you think that Kolchak's right? Aren't we fighting our own?* And some days I myself feel like a sheep, I don't understand anything. There are feuds everywhere! One doctor in Tomsk, a decent man, told me about you, that you have been paid big money by the Japanese since 1905. And there was that prisoner, a wounded Kolchak marine, who proved to us that Lenin was playing into the hands of the Germans. He had documents and they showed that Lenin had been corresponding with German generals about money. I had him shot so he wouldn't bother our people, but all the same I was long troubled in my heart. Nothing is straightforward, who are you to believe? Everybody is against everyone else. You're frightened even to believe yourself'.

I have had many conversations with peasants on various subjects, and the general impression they have made on me is depressing: people see much, but understand desperately little. In particular, the conversations about the holy relics showed me that the exposure of the church's deceit strengthened the suspicious and distrustful attitude of the countryside to the town; not to the clergy, not to authority, but simply to the town as a complex organisation of cunning people who live on the labour and grain of the countryside and make many things useless to the peasant whom they strive in every way to deceive, and skilfully do so.

When working on the commission for the liquidation of illiteracy, I once discussed with a group of peasants from just outside Petersburg the question of scientific and technological advances.

'Yes,' said one listener, a fine-looking, bearded man, 'we have learnt to fly in the air like jackdaws, to swim under the water like pike, but we don't know how to live on the earth. We should first set ourselves up properly on the earth, and the air can wait till afterwards. And money should not be wasted on these antics!'

Another one added angrily: 'These tricks are no use to us, but it's a great expense in people and money. I need horseshoes, an axe, I haven't any nails and there you are putting up monuments in the streets—it's sheer indulgence!'

'There are no clothes for the kids, and you're hanging out flags everywhere . . .'

Then in conclusion, after long, fierce criticism of urban 'antics', a bearded muzhik said with a sigh: 'If we had made the revolution ourselves, there would long since have been peace and quiet on the earth. . . '

Sometimes the attitude to townsmen finds a simple, but radical form of expression: 'All the educated people must be cleared off the earth, then we fools can live easily, otherwise you'll wear us out!'

In 1919 the nicest countryman quietly took the townsman's shoes, his clothes, and generally fleeced him, bartering grain and potatoes for anything necessary or unnecessary for the countryside.

I am reluctant to speak of the crude taunting, the vengeful mockery with which the village greeted the hungry people of the town.

While always gaining on the exchange, the majority of peasants endeavoured and knew how to impose on it a humiliating tone of charity reluctantly bestowed upon the gentleman 'who has squandered his means on the revolution'. It was noticeable that they dealt with workers, if not as with a human being, at least more circumspectly. Probably this caution is explained by the anecdotal advice of one peasant to another: 'You go a bit careful with him, they say he served on a Soviet somewhere'.

A member of the intelligentsia was almost inevitably subjected to moral torment. For example, having established, after a long argument, the precise terms of the exchange, the muzhik or his wife would calmly tell the man whose children at home were suffering from scurvy: 'No, God go with you. We've changed our minds, you can't have the potatoes. . . '

When a man complained that he had to wait too long, he would receive the unforgiving reply: 'We used to wait still longer for your favours'.

Whatever his other characteristics, magnanimity is not a distinguishing feature of the Russian peasant. We can say of him that he is not vindictive: he does not remember the evil he has done to others, nor does he remember the good done him by others.

A certain engineer, disturbed by the peasants' attitude to a group of townsmen who had made their way into the countryside in the autumn rain, and were for long unable to find a place to dry themselves and have a rest, this engineer, working in this village on the peat-cuttings, made a speech to the peasants on the historical services of the intelligentsia in the political liberation of the people. A blue-eyed Slav with light brown hair drily replied: 'We have read that your lot have really suffered quite a bit for your politics, but then that is your affair. You know, you turned to revolution of your own will; we didn't hire you—so we're not to answer for your sorrows—God will settle his account with you for everything . . .'

I would not quote these words, if I did not consider them typical—in various contexts I have heard them myself dozens of times.

But it is essential to note that the humbling of the cunning townsmen before the countryside was of great and instructive significance for it: the countryside clearly understood that the town depended on it, while until this moment it had only felt its own dependence on the town.

*   *   *

An unprecedented, terrible famine rages in Russia, it is killing tens of thousands and will kill millions. This drama evokes sympathy even among those hostile to Russia, a country where, in the words of an American woman, 'There is always cholera or revolution'. What is the attitude of the Russian peasant who is still comparatively well-fed to this drama?

'They don't weep in Ryazan' for a harvest failure in Pskov' he replies, in the words of an old proverb.

'People die, the road is made smooth for us', an old Novgorod man said to me, and his son, a good-looking student at a military school, expanded his father's thought: 'The misfortune is a vast one and many people will die. But who will die? Those weak and worn out by life; for those who survive it will be five times easier'. That is the voice of the genuine Russian peasant, to whom the future belongs. Men of this type reflect calmly and very cynically, they feel their strength and importance.

'You don't run the muzhik', they say. 'The muzhik has now understood: he who has the grain in his hands holds authority and power'.

This is the view of the peasants who 'greeted the policy of nationalisation by a reduction in sowings just enough to leave the urban population without grain and deprive the authorities of a single ear of grain for export abroad'.**

'The muzhik is like a forest: you burn and chop him down, but he grows and grows again of himself,' I was told by a peasant who had come from Voronezh to Moscow in September for books on agriculture. 'We haven't noticed that the war reduced the number of people. But now, they say, millions will die—of course, that will be noticeable. If you count only two *desya-*

tinas a corpse, how much land will that free? There you are. Then we'll show you such work the whole world will be amazed. The muzhik knows how to work, only give him the wherewithal. He doesn't go on strike—the land won't let him!'

In general, the well-fed and not so well-fed peasants regard the tragedy of the famine calmly, as they have been accustomed to regard natural calamities from ancient times. As for the future, the peasants look on it now with increasing confidence, and in the tone in which they are beginning to speak, you feel men who recognise themselves as the sole real master of the Russian land.

A man from Ryazan' explained to me a very curious system of regional economy. 'We don't need large factories, my friend, they only mean riots and all sorts of vice. We would do it like this: a fulling mill with about a hundred workers, a leather works—also quite small, and so we would have all small factories, and further apart, so that workers shouldn't gather together in one place; and so we would smoothly cover the whole *guberniya* with small factories, and the next *guberniya* in the same way. Everyone would have his own, no-one would go in need of anything. The worker would be well-fed, and also everyone would be calm. Workers are greedy, they want everything they see, but the muzhik is satisfied with little.'

'Do many think like that?' I asked. 'Some do, the wiser ones'. 'You don't like the workers?' 'Why? I only say they are a restless people when there is a great crowd of them. We have to break them up into little artels, a hundred here, a hundred there . . .'

The peasants' attitude to the Communists is expressed, in my opinion, most candidly and precisely in the advice given by his fellow villagers to a talented peasant poet of my acquaintance. 'You watch you don't join the commune, Ivan, or we'll cut the throats of your father and brother, and of the neighbours of both of them as well'. 'Why the neighbours?' 'We must root out your spirit'.

*   *   *

What, then, are my conclusions.

First, hatred of meanness and stupidity should not be taken as a lack of friendly concern for man, although meanness and stupidity do not exist outside of man. I have sketched, as I understand it, the environment in which the tragedy of the Russian revolution has been and is being played out. It is an environment of semi-savage people.

I explain the cruel manifestations of the revolution in terms of the exceptional cruelty of the Russian people.

When the leaders of the revolution, a group of the most active members of the intelligentsia, are accused of 'brutality', I regard these accusations as lies and slander inevitable in the struggle of political parties, or, among upright people, as honest error.

I would recall that at all times and everywhere the lies of the aggrieved and vanquished take on particularly evil and shameless forms. It by no means follows from this that I consider the truth of the victors sacred and unchallengeable. No, I simply want to say something of which I am very conscious and which may be mildly expressed in words of a sad, but veritable truth: whatever ideas may guide them, people in their practical activity still remain beasts, often frenzied ones, and the frenzy is sometimes explicable by fear. Accusations of egotistic self-interest, ambition and dishonesty I consider altogether inapplicable to any one of the groups of the Russian intelligentsia; all who bandy such accusations about are well aware that they are unfounded.

I am not denying that politicians are the most sinful among all accused sinners on this earth, but this is because the nature of their activity inexorably obliges them to follow the Jesuitical principle that 'the aim justifies the means'.

But true lovers and fanatics of ideas often deliberately distort their feelings for the good of others. This is particularly true of the majority of the active Russian intelligentsia; it has always subordinated the question of the quality of life to the interests and demands of the quantity of primitive men.

I cannot consider those who took on themselves the hard, the Herculean labour of cleansing the Augean stables of Russian life as 'tormentors of the people', to me they are rather its victims. I say this on the basis of the firmly-held conviction that the whole of the Russian intelligentsia, which for almost a whole century has manfully attempted to set on its feet the ponderous Russian people, lying lazily, negligently and lucklessly on its soil—the whole intelligentsia is a historical victim of a people vegetating on a fabulously rich land on which it managed to live astonishingly poorly. The Russian peasant, whose common sense has now been awakened by the revolution, might say of his intelligentsia: stupid as the sun, it, too, works for no reward.

Of course he will not say this, for he does not yet understand the critical importance of intellectual labour. Almost the whole store of intellectual energy accumulated by Russia in the nineteenth century has been expended by the revolution and dissolved in the peasant mass.

The member of the intelligentsia, the producer of the bread of the spirit, the worker, the creator of the mechanism of urban culture, these are gradually and with ever-growing rapidity being engulfed by the peasantry, who greedily suck up all that is useful to them in the achievements of these four years of furious work.

We can now say with certainty that the Russian peasantry has come alive at the price of losing the intelligentsia and the working class.

Yes, the cost to the muzhik has been great, and he has not yet paid the full price, the tragedy is not ended. But the revolution, carried out by a numerically insignificant group of the intelligentsia at the head of several thousand workers it had educated—this revolution has furrowed the whole mass of the people with a steel plough so deeply that the peasantry can scarcely return to the old forms of life which have been reduced to dust forever; like the Jews that Moses led out of Egyptian slavery, the half-savage, stupid, ponderous people of the Russian villages and hamlets—all those almost terrible people of whom we spoke—will die out, and a new tribe will take their place—literate, sensible, hearty people.

In my view this will not be a very 'nice and likeable Russian people', but this will be finally a businesslike people, distrustful of and indifferent to everything which is not directly related to its needs.

It will be a long time before they ponder Einstein's theory or learn to understand the importance of Shakespeare or Leonardo da Vinci, but they will probably give money for Shteinach's experiments, and undoubtedly will very quickly understand the value of electricity, the value of trained agricultural officers, the usefulness of the tractor, the need to have a good doctor in every village and the use of highways.

They will develop a good historical memory and, remembering their recent tormented past, in the first stages of building a new life they will be rather distrustful of, if not outright hostile to, the intelligentsia and the workers who cause various disorders and revolts.

The town, the inextinguishable hearth of a demanding and ever-exploring thought, the source of stimulating events and phenomena, not always comprehended, will not quickly earn a just evaluation from this man; he will not be quick to see it as a workshop where new ideas, machines, things are continually made, intended to lighten and embellish the people's life.

That is the scheme of my impressions and thoughts on the Russian people.

NOTES

* In Siberia, in Kustanai, a detachment of peasant partisans went over from the Bolsheviks to Kolchak and vice versa twenty-one times.

** From the speech of L. Kamenev at the IX Congress of Soviets, December 1921.

The Soviet Countryside
1917–1924

Its economics and life

by

A. M. Bol'shakov

WORKERS' PUBLISHING HOUSE PRIBOI, LENINGRAD, 1924

Contents

Translated in this work—TMM, REFS.

An Average Farm, its Income and the Family Budget

It now seems to me essential to describe an average farm for the *volost'*, together with its income and approximate budget, in order to have a clearer conception of the economic aspects of life in the *volost'* and to make a better approach to the materials in the subsequent part of the work. This description does not follow from theoretical computations and considerations; it results from studying real and typical farms in the *volost'* and particular budget data for some families, also typical, for 1920.

The family comprises: three able-bodied members (aged 16 years or over) and three others (a child under 5 and two children between 5 and 16).

The land: $2\frac{1}{2}$ *desyatinas* of arable land in all three fields (winter sown, spring sown and fallow); about 7 *desyatinas* of hayfield, mainly on wastes and by marshes; $\frac{1}{10}$th *desyatina* of garden by the house; we leave out pastures, forest and other land, as not immediately relevant to our description.

Livestock and poultry: a horse, cow and calf, two ewes and their lambs, ten hens and a cockerel.

The farm is run without hired help and without the use of any agricultural machinery.

GROSS INCOME OF THE FARM

In determining the income we shall have in mind two harvest rates: the average and the 1920 harvest, which (apart from grasses) was considerably above average.

1. Field crops.

TABLE I

Amount (puds)

	Sown	Average harvest	1920 harvest
Rye	8	43·2	64
Oats	12	38·4	42
Potatoes	25	135	150
Flax, seed	1·5	3·5	7·5
fibre		4·8	4·5

2. Livestock and poultry products. The cow will give 60 *puds* of milk a year; this agrees with the figure given by Vargin [*1912: 15*]. Five *puds* of milk go to feed the calf. Estimating that two ewes have on average three lambs a year and that these are killed at 8-10 months, we will get 2 *puds* 10 pounds of meat a year. In addition, in three years two 6-8 month calves are killed and give 1 *pud* 20 pounds of meat a year. The third calf covers the loss of the cow from old age, disease and death. The total meat on the farm will be about 3 *puds* 30 pounds. Sheepskins are used for warm winter clothing and the wool, amounting to about 9 pounds a year, is used for felt footwear. Ten chickens give 800 eggs a year; five can be killed and replaced by young birds; this gives about 12 pounds of chicken meat.

3. Garden produce. Over the year we obtain: 15 *puds* of cabbage, 3 *puds* of

cucumbers, $1\frac{1}{2}$ *puds* of carrots and about 1 *pud* of beetroot, turnips and so on.
4. Feed for livestock. About 460 *puds* of hay is taken from 7 *desyatinas* with
an average harvest, but only 224 *puds* were gathered in 1920. Apart from hay,
the feeds comprise 12 puds of oats, about 54 *puds* of straw from the spring
sown crop, 11 *puds* of chaff and 2 *puds* of oil cake obtained from the production of linseed oil. In accordance with no. 62, art. 683, para. 3 in *Sobranie
Uzakonenii i rasporyazhenii rabochego i krest'yanskogo pravitel'stva za 1918g.*
and the concluding part of this statute empowering Guberniya Food Committees to reduce the rate indicated in art. 3 (18 *puds*), 12 *puds* of oats per
horse were reserved in Tver' *guberniya* for 1920. In weight, the straw from
the spring sown crop came to about $1\frac{1}{2}$ times the grain, and from rye about
twice; about 7 pounds of chaff are obtained per *pud* of grain. If there is a
shortage of these feeds, the farmer will add rye straw as well; there is about
128 *puds* of it, usually used as litter for the livestock.
5. Manure on the farm. The amount of manure on the farm is of extreme
importance for its income, since manure contains all the substances entering
into the composition of plants and, spread on the land as fertiliser, returns to
it all that was extracted in growing the rye, oats and so on. Our farm will have
about 1,320 *puds* of manure.

FARM EXPENDITURE

1. Field crops. Let us make a calculation bearing in mind the 1920 harvest,
which was much above average. The farm dealt with will not be far from a
critical state with an average harvest of grain, potatoes and flax. A lower than
average harvest means disaster; part of the livestock has to be got rid of, the
members of the family have to seek earnings on the side, etc. Calculations for
average and below average harvest will confirm this.

TABLE 2

Expenditure of field crops (puds)—*harvest of 1920*

	Rye	Oats	Potatoes	Flax seed	Flax fibre
Seed	8	12	25	$1\frac{1}{2}$	—
Compulsory appropriation	$5\frac{3}{8}$	12	$6\frac{1}{4}$	$1\frac{1}{5}$	1
Family's food (1)	$50\frac{2}{8}$	6	108	$4\frac{4}{5}$	—
For the horse	—	12	—	—	—
Family needs	—	—	—	—	$3\frac{1}{4}$
For the calf, chickens (2)	—	—	$10\frac{3}{4}$	—	—
Total	64	42	150	$7\frac{1}{4}$	$4\frac{1}{4}$

Notes: (1) If their own rye crop was sufficient, family needs had to be satisfied with up to 12 *puds*
per person per year (half that for children under five). Anything over was taken away. If fewer than 9
puds could be provided for each member of the family for the year, the family would be allowed
30 pounds (of grain or flour) per month for each member (half this for children under 5) from its
own stock. When a family had eaten its grain, it became entitled to a 'hunger ration' of 15 pounds
per person per month from the Volost' Executive Committee until the next harvest (1 August).
But the rations were not issued consistently: in 1919 they ceased on 1 April; in 1920 on 1 June;
in 1921 distribution was stopped altogether.
(2) Rotting potatoes, usually 8–10 per cent of the harvest, are used.

Three *puds* of oatmeal are obtained from 6 *puds* of oats; 6 *puds* of flax seed are delivered to the oil-mill where the state appropriation is taken; about a *pud* of linseed oil is obtained from the rest. The fibre goes for thread and homespun cloth from which the women make underwear, towels and so on.
2. Livestock and poultry products. The wool is made into felt footwear, as has already been mentioned, the sheepskins go for warm clothing. Later we shall see whether our farm has enough wool and sheepskins, whether all the eggs, milk, meat and so on go to feed the family, or whether the head of the family exchanges part of these products for salt, sugar, etc. We express the butter tax of 2 pounds in terms of milk, reckoning that 1 *pud* of butter is produced from 35 *puds* of milk [*Vargin, 1912: 18*].

TABLE 3

Expenditure of livestock and poultry products

	Meat (*puds*)	Milk (*puds*)	Eggs	Chicken meat (*pounds*)	Wool (*pounds*)	Sheep-skins
Compulsory appropriations by the state	1½	1¾	10	⅔	2	½
Family's food	2¼	53¼	770	11⅓	—	—
To raise chickens	—	—	20	—	—	—
Family needs	—	—	—	—	—	2½
For the calf	—	5	—	—	—	—
Total	3¾	60	800	12	9	3

Note: Cream, cheese and butter are not included in the table, we assume, for convenience, that milk was consumed unprocessed.

3. Garden produce. Garden produce is not liable to appropriation by the state. Dried carrots serve as a substitute for tea (other village substitutes for tea are: dried apple leaves, strawberry leaves, pounded roast grains of rye, etc.). Dried beetroot replaces sugar (tobacco was sown in gardens in 1920; the harvest was good, but the processing, drying and so on was not always successful).
4. Feed for livestock. The number of fodder units required for all stock for the stalled period (1 October to 20 April, Old Style, or from the beginning of October to the beginning of May, New Style) is 7,338. According to Prido-rogin [*1896: 36-8*] and Vargin [*1912: 13-15*], the fodder unit requirements for average peasant livestock per annum are: 4,992 for a horse, 3,080 for a cow; 1,050 for a ewe and her lambs. During the stalled period the horse needs 2,772 units, the cow 3,080, the ewe and lambs 573. The remainder of the time the stock will be on pasture. Nevertheless, it is essential to give the horses not less than 246 fodder units in addition to pasturage during the spring and autumn tillage. So, 7,584 fodder units of feed are required for the stock. But on the basis of the 1920 harvest we only have 5,662 fodder units, counting the hay (18 units a *pud*), oats (40 units), straw from the spring crop (16 units), chaff (11 or 12 units) and oil cake (77 units). We are about 1,922 units short. If the farmer added all the rye straw, this would give only

1,152 units. But he cannot do this, since the stock must have litter (and to get manure, litter is essential); at least 110 *puds* go on litter although, according to agricultural advisers, the litter for our farm should be not less than 140 *puds* [Vargin, 1912 : 13]. The remaining 18 *puds* of rye straw will give 162 units. Thus, there will still be a shortage of 1,750 fodder units. The only way out of the critical feed situation is to sell the calf. From the autumn of 1920 the peasants offered their milch cows on the following conditions to those who were willing to take them : in return for feeding the cow they could make free use of its milk from 1 October to 20 April, but when the cattle were driven to pasture on 20 April, the cow was to be returned to its owner. But there were few takers; there was nowhere to get feed. So, in the autumn and winter of 1920, very many farms sold part of their livestock. In 1921 there will be considerably fewer farm animals in the *volost'* than in the preceding year.

5. Manure on the farm. Our farmer has $2\frac{1}{2}$ *desyatinas* of arable land, i.e. $\frac{5}{6}$ *desyatina* in each field. Manure is needed only for the spring field and the area under potatoes; there is $\frac{1}{5}$ *desyatina* under potatoes. So one *desyatina* is to be manured. We find then that the manure will be insufficient: it will be 155 *puds* short of the *uezd* norm (1,475 in 1912-13) and 1,650 *puds* short of the amount suggested for a *desyatina* of arable by agricultural advisers. So, in order to manure the land at the rate advised, our average farm should have twice as many livestock as it actually has. But the feedstuffs, as we have seen, do not always allow the present livestock to be fed. Consequently, the question is on the agenda for replacing the three-field by a multi-field rotation, which would reduce the fallow area; and for increasing, or rather introducing, sown grasses which would allow a greater number of stock to be maintained; or, finally, using artificial manure.

THE BUDGET

'The budget is a microscope which enables us to glimpse what is concealed beneath the complexities and confusions of family relations' [*Shcherbina, 1900: introduction*]. The first works on peasant budgets appeared at the end of the 1870s (P. P. Semenov) and at the very beginning of the 1880s (E. N. Anuchin); see the introduction to Shcherbina's book for a history of peasant budgets. But it is impossible to deduce data for the average budget of a Russian peasant, since the investigations were carried out in different areas of Russia at different times and with widely varied programmes. Shcherbina calls a budgetary inventory of property in the budget 'an image of the economic structure of the country concerned' and includes in it all property, from the land and buildings down to the tiniest items of domestic equipment. We are concerned with the peasant's budget only incidentally and so understand it more narrowly. We have tried to include in the budget what, on the one hand, an average peasant in the *volost'* bought for his family and farm and what, on the other, he sold in order to be able to buy necessities.

Usually the peasants now only buy what is difficult or impossible to make on the farm; in peasant life of recent years there has been almost no buying and selling, it has been replaced by barter, but for convenience we shall ascribe a money price to everything acquired or disposed of.

Here we shall quote the average sales and purchases of various products on a peasant farm in Tver' *guberniya,* based on records for 223 farms in 1908 [*Statisticheskii ezhegodnik po Tverskoi gubernii za 1908g., 1910: 283-311*], and data for an average farm in our *volost'* in 1920.

TABLE 4

Sales

Sales	1908		1920	
	puds	*rubles*	*puds*	*rubles*
Bread grains	14·2	13·59		
Potatoes	6·6	2·22	10	55,000
Other products of fields, meadows and gardens (6 puds of oats and 1½ puds of fibre in 1920)	45·3	56·59	7·5	201,000
Firewood and forestry products		9·41		
Cattle		16·47		
Other livestock and domestic poultry		3·37		40,000
Meat		1·12	1	20,000
Leather, sheepskins and wool		2·30		
Eggs (number)		1·12	700	140,000
Butter, milk and other dairy produce		5·82	1	200,000
Honey and wax		1·14		
Canvas, thread and domestic products		3·35		
Total sold		116·50		656,000
				or 65·6 gold rubles in 1920

The sale of 6 *puds* of oats meant that the feed stock was thus reduced by a further 240 fodder units. The 1920 paper unit was worth 0.0001 gold rubles.

For 1908 the overexpenditure on the farm amounted to 145 rubles 16 kopeks. This was met by earnings from off-farm crafts and trades. In 1920 the overexpenditure on our farm was 35,875 rubles (or 3 rubles 59 kopeks in gold). The farm also has a number of small expenditures: payments at fixed prices for products allocated to it through the shop (manufactured goods, paraffin etc.), for contributions to the church and so on; I do not include these expenditures since they, and the overexpenditure for 1920, are partly covered by receipts (at fixed prices) for produce appropriated by the state and by petty earnings (e.g. helping a neighbour at threshing) and so on.

The figures given for the 1920 budget are not an arithmetic mean obtained by surveying a series of separate family budgets. It has never been an easy job to give an account of the income and expenditure of a peasant family, because peasants are chary about questions about their money matters, but today, in 1920, every family carefully conceals its financial situation not merely from the stranger, but even from neighbours, fearful of being called to account for what it has sold, of the introduction of new taxes and so on. I have described the income and expenditure of only one family whose particulars I know well; some figures in this budget have been amended with the help of fragmentary information from the budgets of some other families.

TABLE 5
Purchases

| | 1908 | | 1920 | |
	puds	rubles	puds	rubles
Rye, malting barley, oats	19·4	25·69		
Wheat flour	4·8	11·86		
Various grits	7·8	15·02		
Potatoes	1·9	0·86		
Cabbages, cucumbers, onions	5·6	2·65		
Flax and vegetable seeds	0·7	4·46		6,000
Hay, straw, cake	19·7	3·46		
Cattle and domestic poultry		7·30		
Meat, fat and Russian butter	1·5	5·99		
Fish	1·20	4·23		
Salt	6·2	2·16	2·5	120,000
Vegetable oil		1·95		
Sugar, spices, sweetmeats (pounds)	134·3	17·56	8	32,000
Tea (pounds)	6·3	9·94		
Vodka (vedros)	6·1	13·58		
Hops (pounds)		1·46	2	8,000
Tobacco (pounds)	9·1	2·28	1	10,000
Firewood		3·74		
Paraffin	2·3	3·51	0·5	20,000
Other lighting		2·19		
Soap (pounds)	23·8	2·89	12	48,000
Furniture		0·69		
Kitchen ware and crockery		6·34		3,375
Books, luxury items, etc.		4·29		
Clothing		32·68		117,500
Footwear		21·92		186,000
Various cloth, textiles		11·26		
Building materials, nails, etc.		15·11		7,500
Ploughs, sokhas, harrows		4·06		21,000
Carts, wheels, wood-sledges		8·84		60,000
Scythes, sickles, bars, spades		1·88		10,000
Dung forks and spades		0·45		
Cart and carriage harness		4·92		37,500
Threshers, winnowers, etc.		4·39		
Domestic implements		2·05		5,000
Total		261·66		691,875
				or 69·19 gold rubles in 1920

Let me explain certain figures in this budget.

Purchases: two half ounces of vegetable seed at 3,000 rubles a half ounce; 8 pounds of sugar intended almost exclusively for guests; the kitchenware acquired was one earthenware cooking pot and two milk jugs; each jug was exchanged for a couple of eggs and the pot for 10 pounds of potatoes; the clothing acquired was a half-length plush winter overcoat for the 16 year old girl in exchange for half a *pud* of butter, a short jacket from their own sheepskin for the boy made up in the house by a tailor who also spent two days mending old clothes; as for footwear, in the autumn a pair of leather boots were bought for 65,000 rubles, six pairs of soles for 72,000 rubles, boot repairs cost 15,000 rubles, two pairs of sandals for 8,000 rubles (5,000 rubles for leather and 3,000 rubles for the work), two pairs of felt boots for which their own wool (7 pounds) was not enough and another three pounds had to be bought; 5 pounds of nails were bought at 1,500 rubles a pound; the plough, sokhas, harrows entry covers the following: two shares for 8,000 rubles, reforging the plough sole 500 rubles; sharpening the teeth of the harrow 2,500 rubles; a major repair to the mouldboard of the plough 10,000 rubles; the carts, wheels, wood sledges entry covers: fitting tyres to wheels 10,000 rubles, purchase of new wood sledge for 50,000 rubles; under the next entry, one scythe was bought for 10,000 rubles; no new harness items were acquired; but 15,000 rubles were paid to tan a hide to be used for harness repairs (they carried out the repairs themselves); 30 pounds of tar cost 15,000 rubles and $2\frac{1}{2}$ pounds of nails for shoeing the horses, 5,000 rubles, and 2,500 rubles were spent on shoeing the horse (five times); as for domestic implements, an axe was bought for 5,000 rubles.

All this was essential expenditure. Someone unacquainted with everyday life in the countryside might perhaps find the purchase of an overcoat (the plush coat) for the girl unnecessary; but our girl is beginning to 'dress up', as they say in Tver' *guberniya*, or 'to become a bride'; she cannot go 'walking out' with young fellows in a sheepskin coat, they would avoid her, not invite her to dances, etc.; circumstances forced their hand and, hard though it was on the family budget, an overcoat had to be acquired.

Let us call attention to the fact that a whole series of articles which would certainly have been acquired in peace time, are now completely lacking among the peasants; for example, vodka, tea, wheat flour (rolls were baked for visitors at the major annual festivals), buckwheat and wheat flakes etc. The consumption of other items has been considerably reduced: approximately 73 per cent less salt per person is used than in peacetime, 64 per cent less soap, etc.

The gross income of our average farm (excluding the value of manure) is 4,718,357 rubles, or 471 rubles 84 kopeks in gold; we are speaking of 1920, I would remind you. It comprises the following items of income which are given as percentages of the gross income and compared with the correspond-

TABLE 6

	Our average farm	Russia
Income from:		
grain[a]	50.6	43.7
livestock	13.1	27.7
feedstuffs[b]	35.2	23.8
garden produce	1.1	6.8
	100	100[c]

NOTES

a 'Grain' includes income from flax and potatoes.
b Apart from hay and straw from spring-sown crops and rye, 'feedstuffs' includes chaff and cake.
c This in fact sums to 102—*TMM, REFS.*

ing figures for peasant farms in Russia taken from an article on the peasant
farm [*Polnaya entsiklopediya russkago sel'skogo khozyaistva, IV: 1013*],
to show the changes which have taken place in the components of gross
income of the average peasant farm.

We see that the share of income from field crops has risen somewhat (6.9
per cent), compared with the peacetime level. In part, the peasant has tried
to increase the arable area, so far as the area of suitable land, the state of his
livestock and equipment and the availability of family labour allowed him to;
he has tilled some strip, or a patch beyond the fields which formerly ran to
waste. In part, though, the income under this entry has increased owing to
more careful tillage: he is tilling deeper, has carried out an additional harrow-
ing and so on. This behaviour is understandable: the peasant has to provide
himself with grain; he must try to build up a small surplus from the field
crops to meet the pressing needs of the family and the farm. The income
from livestock products is now smaller than in peacetime. This is quite understandable. The growth of population and of the number of farms has considerably outstripped the increase in cattle and small livestock.[1] This is true
for the *volost'* as a whole:

TABLE 7

	Population		Farms		Horses		Cattle		Sheep		Pigs	
	no.	%	no.	%	no.	%	no.	%	no.	%	no.	%
1916	7068	100	1455	100	1821	100	3074	100	1410	100	192	100
1920	9676	137	1836	126	1477	81	3830	125	2664	189	7	4
1923	9216	130	1883	129	1562	86	4094	132	3204	227	92	48

This is also true for the average farm which in peacetime would have had more
small animals and, in some years perhaps, would even have had a couple of
cows. The relative increase in income from feedstuffs is due to the increased
price of hay (in 1920 a *pud* cost 60 kopeks in gold, compared with 30 in
peacetime). The garden income declined because of the poor vegetable harvest in 1920.

Let us compare the average consumption of bread and of potatoes, the
basic foods, for each family member for a year. An average peasant family
of Voronezh *guberniya* in the 1890s had: 16 *puds* 17.5 pounds of bread and
3 *puds* 14.4 pounds of potatoes, according to Shcherbina [*1900: 433*]. The
Goritsy *volost'* farm consumed: 8 *puds* 29 pounds of bread, 18 *puds* of
potatoes. In calculating the amount of bread, a weight increase of 33 per cent
has been assumed. The high consumption of potatoes per person is explained
by the sharp decline in the consumption of bread, as well as of meat, butter,
etc., which has made the potato the main item of peasant diet.

Comparative Burden of Taxation on the Land

To put the present burden of taxation on the land in proper perspective, we
shall now try to make some historical comparisons of the burden of various

forms of direct taxes on peasant land (including rent, in whatever form paid for land). Since a substantial part of a peasant's agricultural income derives from field crops, we shall relate all direct taxes incident on different types of land to one only, that is arable land; and thus it is of particular interest to show, in historical perspective, what percentage of the gross income from land direct taxation represents.

We shall consider the following periods or points in time:

the sixteen century, when the economic basis for the subsequent legal institution of serfdom was being laid down;

the year 1614, during the Time of Troubles, when the collapse of the state machinery meant, according to Veselovskii [*1915, I: 39*], that the ability of the population to pay was stretched to the limits, while, at the same time, legalised serfdom had crystallised sufficiently to enable landlords to exploit peasant labour to the full; Klyuchevskii considers the decree (*ukaz*) of 9 March 1607 (on fugitive peasants) 'perhaps the most important act in the legal establishment of serfdom' [*1919: 234*];

the 1840s, when the landlord class, in the persons of its most farsighted representatives, was on the point of recognising the crisis of the economy based on labour rents, according to Pokrovskii [*1913, V: 37-38*], and was making a last attempt to extract from the peasant as much as possible of the fruits of his labours;

the 1870s, when the peasantry, left to its own devices, clashed with the capitalist system of the state economy;

the period 1892-1903, when our industry was making great strides and drawing a certain part of the agricultural population into the mills and factories, but simultaneously, because it was state-subsidised, was imposing, through the state, an additional burden on peasant landholding; in 1866 in European Russia there were 734,971 workers employed in manufacturing industries [*Nikolay -on, 1893, Table II*]; fifteen years later, by 1900, the number was 1,512,317 [*Statisticheskii Ezhegodnik Rossii za 1904g.: 264-77*];

the year 1915, one of the years after the abolition of redemption payments and also a year just preceding the revolution; and, finally,

the years 1918-23, when general historical conditions had made the countryside the base for the construction of the government's economic policy.

All the data for these periods can be summarised in Table 8:

A few comments are needed to interpret this table properly.

For the sixteenth century there is ample carefully researched material in the works of Professor N. A. Rozhkov. Our average peasant arable area is derived from his data [*1920 : 40-79*]. Lappo [*1894: 25*] and Sergeevich [*1911, III: 337*] indicate roughly the same area per peasant household, but it should be noted that Rozhkov [*1899: 144*], Milyukov [*1892: 108*], Veselovskii and others indicate larger areas of peasant arable land than those which became typical, especially in the central regions, in the later part of the sixteenth century. Veselovskii [*1915, I: 2*] states that the unit of assessment for dues in kind was the *vyt'*, thus indicating that originally the

TABLE 8

Time	Region	(i) Average peasant arable land in 3 fields (desyatinas)	(ii) Gross income from 1 desyatina (peacetime rubles)	(iii) Direct taxes per 1 desyatina of arable land (peacetime rubles)	Taxes as percentage of gross income (iii) as percentage of (ii)
16th century	Central	3.75	47.6	25.05	53
1614	Vologda uezd	unknown	87.8	48.16	55
1840s	Ryazan' gub.	6.0	50.79	12.0	24
1870s	Tver' gub.	2.98	44.09	12.72	29
1892–1903	Central	2.31	44.09	9.74	22
1915	Goritsy volost'	4.29	42.03	4.96	12
1918	Ditto	3.62	42.03	2.18	5
1919	Ditto	3.54	42.03	3.62	9
1920	Ditto	3.96	61.44	8.24	13 (19)
1921	Ditto	3.88	79.72	8.63	11 (21)
1922	Ditto	3.84	48.34	5.58	12
1923	Ditto	3.81	44.33	4.16	9

vyt' was an indivisible economic unit, representing a peasant family's land-tilling capacity. We determined the gross income from data on the productivity of the soil, the average price of grain in the sixteenth century, and the average value of the sixteenth-century ruble in terms of present-day money [*Rozhkov, 1899: 259, 210, 234; Rozhkov, 1920: 77; Klyuchevsky, 1959 b: 183*]. The various state taxes are listed by Rozhkov, and we have taken the landlord's income to be one half of the crop, whether it was actually paid as a share of the crop, in the form of a grain rent (*posopnyi khleb*—one of the forms of sixteenth century quit-rent: a specified quantity of grain was exacted from a given area of arable land), in money, or as a combination of any of these. Rozhkov [*1899: 230 and 1920: 77, 78*] claims that 'while reducing the rent in the form of a set share of the harvest, the landlords raised the rents in grain and in money and these increases fully compensated for the decrease in the set share'.

The arable area in 1614 is not known (for the Vologda *uezd*), but we can safely assume it to have been similar to that for the sixteenth century in the Central regions. Although, in general, the arable area in the Northern region was even smaller than in the Central area, for the early seventeenth century, when the 'Time of Troubles' pushed the peasants into the north, too, the average arable land in the Northern region can be taken as 3.75 *desyatinas*. The gross income has been calculated using the sixteenth-century figure for soil productivity [*Rozhkov, 1899: 168*]. Rozhkov notes [*1899: 259*] that sixteenth-century soil productivity was somewhat higher than nowadays, consequently it could not have changed sharply in the seventeenth century. The high income is explained by high grain prices at the beginning of the seventeenth century: grain had become five times dearer compared with its price in the second half of the sixteenth century. The value of money has, of course, been recalculated in terms of present-day money, according to Klyuchevskii's method [*1959b: 161, 183*]. The burden of taxation was calculated as follows: as for earlier periods, we assigned half the income to the landlord, who was now oppressing the peasant even harder than in the previous century; all the other taxes were calculated by reference to the documents quoted by Veselovskii [*1915, I: 407, appendix 5*].

We have chosen, as typical of the 1840s, the estate of a Ranenburg landowner, the not-unknown Colonel Semenov. A description of Semenov's estate is contained in Volkonskii [*1897, vol. XII, Nos. 2 and 3*]; Semenov is also mentioned, incidentally, by Petr Struve [*1913: 131, footnote*]. Semenov drew up a 'Regulation' representing a comprehensive set of rules for a more effective exploitation of peasant labour. The peasant arable land and the yield are taken from Volkonskii [*1897, No. 2: 126, 145*]. The 1840s ruble has been expressed in present-day values by relating the price of rye in the 1840s, given by P. Struve [*1913: 116*], to its modern (pre-war) price, assuming the price of oats to be 75 per cent of that of rye. We have taken the 1825 price of rye and augmented it according to M. N. Pokrovskii [*1913, V: 43*].

Volkonskii calculates the overall value of labour rents as 36 silver rubles per peasant unit (*tyaglo*); he states [*1897, No. 2: 130*] the rent was 18 silver rubles per peasant unit; but serf rents in the form of labour brought the landlord more than 18 rubles. Semenov considered 18 rubles to be the value of the winter haulage performed by a peasant unit, but the summer work was worth more'. We used this figure in determining the impositions on a *desyatina* of arable land, with allowance for the relative values of the ruble in the 1840s and now.

For the 1870s, we obtained the area of usable land per household in the Tver' *guberniya* from Fortunatov [*1893: 72-73*] and Yanson [*1887: 13, 24*], while the area under tillage was calculated from data for the Goritsy *volost'*; the income from the land was calculated by using the yield ratio employed for the last period, the (average) grain prices for the 1870s being taken from Nikolay -on [*1893: Table 9*] (average rye and oats prices) and expressed in modern (pre-war) values. The taxes were calculated by Yanson's method [*1887: 22*], using the same coefficient for the conversion of the ruble that we have just described.

The arable area for 1892-1903 should be approximately equal to that for peasant holdings in the Tver' *guberniya* in the later (pre-war) period, too, since no significant changes in the area of peasant arable land in the Central area have been noted over this comparatively short stretch of time. We derived the arable area from statistical data [*Statisticheskii ezhegodnik po Tverskoi gubernii za 1914-15gg.: 30, 48, 54*]; allotment land and land of private owners was 5 million *desyatinas*, in round figures; the arable land of these categories was used by peasants; the area of arable land has been calculated on the basis of data in *Polnaya entsiklopediya russkogo sel'skogo khozyaistva* [*X: 44*]. There can have been no significant variations in the (gross) income from a *desyatina* compared with that in the 1870s. The taxes are taken from Bogolepov [*: 23*].

For Goritsy *volost'*, the arable area for 1915 not fully sown is, of course, deducted from the overall figure. The gross revenue per *desyatina* has been calculated for both 1918 and 1919 from the average yield and the (average) prices for a variety of crops, including fibre flax. I should point out that I have applied the results calculated for 1918 to both 1915 and 1919. The taxes have been derived from the statistical data [*Statisticheskii ezhegodnik po Tverskoi gubernii za 1914-15gg., 44 and 48*]; insurance payments have been taken as half those of the volost' [*Bogolepov: 25*]. Allowance has been made for the fact that 10 per cent of the total usable land for the *volost'* (excluding forests and pastures) was leased out; for the rent payments we took the average for the guberniya [*Statisticheskii ezhegodnik za 1914-15gg.; 135*].

The figures for the arable area and the gross income for 1918 are self-explanatory. The taxes are derived from figures for the *volost'* expenditure in 1918; the grain appropriated in 1917 we have taken as expenditure for 1918, since in 1917 only an insignificant part of the 8,600 *puds* intended to be appropriated was actually appropriated.

Again, the area under tillage and the income from land in 1919 are clear enough. The tax has been calculated by the same method as for 1918, but since in 1919 the authorities had allocated to the population foodstuffs and other products to the value of 5,438 rubles 63 kopeks at fixed prices (all our calculations are in peacetime currency values), we have deducted this amount from the total of taxation, since it represents a real alleviation of the burden of taxes; but, on the other hand, if allowance is made for this, we should by the same token add to the burden the sum of 798 rubles which was paid by the population for the goods received. All appropriations from the population are fully shown, only the amount distributed in rations being deducted from the total, since this value was something that had been taken away in the first place.

I have performed all the calculations for 1920 analogously to those for the preceding year. The figure '19' shown in brackets in the column 'Taxes as percentage of gross income' shows the burden for 1920, had there been an average harvest in that year instead of an exceptionally large one.

All estimates for 1921, 1922 and 1923 have been made using exactly the same method as for the preceding years of the revolution. If we see that the gross income per *desyatina* of arable land declined for 1922 and 1923, we must look at the harvest. If for the last two years direct taxes per *desyatina* of arable land fell, we must consult the following table [Table 9] where we shall see that recently the state has been taking less from the peasant than it did not so long ago.

It may be useful to mention the source of some figures in the table given above. Let us take, say, the figure for tax per *desyatina* of arable land in 1920. This figure consists almost entirely of the value of agricultural produce compulsorily appropriated by the state; the grain delivery represents, in fact, the bulk of the direct taxes. Objectively, direct taxes are those imposed on income, that is 'taxes on ownership', as Professor I. Kh. Ozerov calls them [*1917:253*]. The total of persons in the *volost'* delivering grain in 1920 was 972; i.e. 53 per cent of all farms in the *volost'* took part in the deliveries. Taking individual cases, a typical average seems to be: $15\frac{1}{2}$ *puds* of rye; $7\frac{1}{2}$ *puds* of oats; $2\frac{1}{2}$ *puds* of barley; a typical minimum was: $2\frac{1}{2}$ *puds* of rye, 5 *puds* of barley; a typical maximum: 86 *puds* of rye, 32 *puds* of oats; 12 *puds* of barley.

Thus, the tax is exacted in kind, in the form of agricultural produce. Let us recall that the present-day peasant lives exclusively from the income of his farm. Yet, before the war and the revolution, in the industrial region (to which Tver' *guberniya* belongs) agriculture gave the peasant only 64 per cent of his annual income [*Polnaya entsiklopediya russkogo sel'skogo khozyaistva, IV:1014*]; the remaining 36 per cent came from off-farm and local crafts and trades (in Goritsy *volost'*: carpentry, winter haulage etc.). In the neighbouring Moscow *guberniya* agriculture gave the peasant even less, 45 per cent [*P. Maslov, 1906 : 346*]. Incidentally, in some *guberniyas*, and particularly Tver', the pre-revolutionary components of income from agriculture were not the same as now (we have already mentioned the pre-war development of flax cultivation in the *guberniya* in general and in Goritsy *volost'* in particular).

TABLE 9

Produce appropriated from the volost' population at fixed prices, money taxes, haulage and labour dues (in puds, unless otherwise stated)

	1917	1918	1919	1920	1921	1922	1923	Total	Returned to the volost population as rations for humans and livestock	Available to the state
Rye, rye flour and barley	8,600	1,938	13,587	19,012	12,154	34,032	26,254	115,577	19,276	96,301
Oats		790	3,929	4,721	6,268			15,708	1,025	14,683
Potatoes		1,200	11,985	18,407	4,776			36,368		36,368
Meat				1,249	575			2,016		2,016
Hay			1,250	5,000	24,633			30,833	1,250	29,633
Straw			1,125	5,346	16,652			23,123	1,650	21,473
Fibre				3,842	1,957			5,799		5,799
Eggs (numbers)				11,880	17,710			29,590		29,590
Butter				112	236			348		348
Flax seed			332	548	1,959			2,839		2,839
Sheepskins				488				488		488
Wool				98	63			161		161
Chickens (live wt)				38	20			58		58
Honey				12	12			24		24
Labour dues (days)			1,210	3,503	3,566			8,279		8,279
Haulage (verstas)				163,392	402,216			565,608		565,608
Money taxes (rubles)		5,016·09	515·57	216·75		1,196·00*				

*In terms of grain price.

A question now arises: in real terms, was the 1920 burden of taxation (13 per cent) lighter than that of 1892–1903 (22 per cent)? The answer must be no. The Ryazan' *guberniya* peasant, with his comparatively large arable area (6 *desyatinas*) and 24 per cent tax burden, was left with more agricultural produce than his fellow from the central region, who had an area little more than a third of his (2.31 *desyatinas*) and a 22 per cent burden (assuming that neither engaged in off-farm crafts and trades, but they lived entirely from their agricultural income, out of which they met their taxes). It is evident that the 1920 peasant who had lost the 34 per cent of his income from crafts and trades, and a certain amount from the cultivation of industrial crops, found it harder to meet his 13 per cent tax burden than he had the former 22 per cent. In particular, in Korcheva *uezd* the peasant derives only 59 per cent of his annual income, not 64 per cent, from agriculture [*Sovremennoe sostoyanie l'novodstva, 126*]. We have, however, used the figure of 64 per cent, since it conforms more closely to the economic situation of Goritsy *volost'* than does the *uezd* figure of 59 per cent.

The transition from an in-kind to a money economy at the end of the sixteenth and in the seventeenth century was accompanied by a profound upheaval in society, was marked by an extreme pathological condition and had an enormous effect on the forms of the economy [*Rozhkov, 1918 : 54 following*]. The reverse phenomenon, the transition from an exchange to an in-kind economy which occurred in the countryside in the early revolutionary period, also had some rather unhealthy manifestations. The point is that, as research shows [*P. Maslov, 1906 : 342 following*], our peasant farm, especially in the industrial region (and particularly in Goritsy *volost'*), basically satisfied only its food requirements; on the consumer nature of the peasant farm see S. Maslov [*1915 : 105*]. Hence the inevitable need for peasant crafts and trades. But the peasant economy was increasingly confined to in-kind forms by the breakdown of the economy, the nationalisation of industry, the abolition of free trade, the extreme restriction of movement within the country, the rapid fall in the value of paper money and so on. Moreover, whereas in former times surplus manpower left agriculture for the mills and factories, thereby increasing the country's total output, now a certain part of this 'surplus work force' has returned again to the countryside, but it is powerless to increase agricultural income by its efforts, given the marginal productvity of the land in this agricultural system.

In 1915, on average 4.29 *desyatinas* of arable land provided food for 5.2 persons; in 1920, 3.54 *desyatinas* also supported 5.2 persons; but these had now been deprived of all their side-earnings. Consequently, they feel the burden of taxation more heavily than before. It is true that for 1920 we do not have to mention the amount of indirect taxation [*Ozerov, 1917 : 253*] which formerly accounted for about 21 per cent of peasant expenditure, according to my calculations for Moscow, Yaroslavl', Kostroma, Novgorod and Vyatka *guberniyas* [*cf. Rozhkov, in Istoriya Rossii v XIVv., VI : 109 etc.*]. In some *guberniyas* in the 1890s indirect taxation was even higher [*Saratovskaya Zemskaya Nedelya, 1903, sentyabr' No 9*]. Yet in 1920, the strain of the war, the destruction, the withdrawal of the work force, the requisitioning of horses, etc. considerably more than offset the improvement in the peasant budget from the abolition of indirect taxes. The population which has flooded into the countryside in recent years is scarcely fit for work; besides, in general the war and all its consequences have undermined the health of the inhabitants of the *volost'*. A relevant fact is that in peacetime the outpatients department of the local hospital averaged no more than 35 patients a day, but now the average is no fewer than 70; there used to be about 15 in-patients, now no fewer than 30 beds are occupied every day.

Thus, what has made the burden of impositions in 1920 heavier is the loss of off-farm crafts and trades and of industrial crops (flax), together with an increased number of mouths in the *volost'* to be fed per unit of arable land.

All the other figures given in the table at the beginning of this chapter [Table 8] could be supplied with detailed comments similar to those I have given for the figure for the burden per *desyatina* of arable land in 1920. In order to avoid excessive detail, though, I confine my comments to 1920, the year when the tax squeeze was most oppressive in the *volost'* I have studied.

At this point I should describe briefly both the principles of taxation, and also the methods of tax collection used during the revolutionary period.

In 1918 the appropriation of alleged surpluses by the state predominated. In that year the state was concerned with only three items: rye, potatoes and oats. For these products the law laid down an annual ration for men and for animals (oats for the horse, flour for feeding calves and cows and so on). Then seed requirements were taken into account. But anything surplus to its ration and seed the farm had to hand over to the state at a fixed price. Farms short of these legal rations, or of seed, had the deficiency made good from the *volost'* fund at a (very low) fixed price. Consequently, if we calculate in terms of rye what the population was supposed to deliver for 1918, we get 3,007 *puds* of rye. Apart from what was to be collected for 1918, the state in that year also took what had been due in 1917 but had not, or practically not, been taken (time ran out since the imposition had been made almost at the end of the year).

For 1917 the *volost'* gathering had decided to exact from the rich 8,600 *puds* of rye at one-fifteenth of the market price. This rye had to be collected with the aid of a Red Army detachment, since many wriggled about to avoid paying their share. In peacetime (1913), however, the *volost'* population used to drink vodka equivalent to almost 40,000 *puds* of rye. In 1918 the state obtained an insignificant amount (and if we deduct the overheads from this insignificant amount—it is unfortunately impossible to calculate—the state was left with a mere crumb for its needs). Remembering just which farms in 1928 paid up and which had no surpluses, I would say that not only poor and middle peasants were registered as having no surpluses, but some of the well-to-do as well. This was because the amount really sown would be concealed, the real harvest reduced and the authorities, still in the process of consolidation, had no chance of verifying what the population declared. Admittedly, rural commissions went round looking at the grain in barns, but, to tell the truth, this was done only 'for form's sake'; and, in any case, only part of the grain was left there, the rest would be carried off (not even hidden) to some other place. Surpluses were carted off to the Executive Committee without coercion.

Surpluses were again collected in 1919. In this year, however, the annual food ration was cut by almost 25 per cent (from 12 *puds* of rye per man per year to 9, etc.). In addition the Committees of the Peasant Poor which had been organised—not over-enthusiastically in some places, it must be said—were pressing to collect more produce. The authorities were now concerned with a wider range of products. Instead of all surpluses being carted to the Executive Committee and then partly distributed as rations, the following procedure was laid down. From the surpluses in a hamlet, annual rations would be issued on the spot to those with shortages. These shortages were often merely formal; in fact a villager, forced to share the fruits of his own labour with a neighbour, knew very well that the other had quite enough grain to last till the next harvest, and so quarrels broke out in the countryside.

'Why should I have to work for you? Starving, are you? You sell the grain, all right, and want to live off others . . .' and so on.

In 1918 there had been no such quarrels, since the group paying surpluses was very restricted, they were mainly the rich. The times were such, though, that the rich preferred to keep quiet rather than draw attention to themselves. In 1919, thanks partly to the reduction in the ration, partly to intimidation by the authorities threatening severe punishment for false declarations of what had been sown (though there was no machinery to check these declarations), the cohort of those paying had greatly increased: many, many middle peasants turned out to have surpluses. Only the bolder and more cunning middle peasant concealed his food stocks and even strove (and many succeeded) to be listed as in need, i.e. entitled to rations. That was where the dissension arose, they swore at one another and denounced one another. The authorities intervened; those pretending to be in need landed in the lock-up; but the 'starving' man in the lock-up was quick to repay those he blamed for his imprisonment; he would have something interesting to tell the authorities about them (absurd or false though it might often be). As a result, ill-will was created in the countryside and neighbour began to fear neighbour. The atmosphere became oppressive in the countryside.

In 1919 the state received more from the *volost'* than it had in the preceding year.

1920 was, as we know, a most difficult year for the state. The civil war was at its height, industry had almost come to a standstill, transport lacked fuel. The country was nearly paralysed. The state could no longer content itself more or less with random surpluses. To survive and fight for its existence it had to have secure, clearly defined resources. As regards the collection of taxation, the principle of surpluses became a thing of the past;

it was replaced by requisitioning. The centre authorities calculated how much of various exactions in their opinion could be collected from the entire country (in our *volost'* 17 items were exacted); this total was broken down or allocated by *guberniyas;* the *guberniyas* made *uezd* allocations taking account of their economic situation; the latter made allocations for each *volost'*, and these for settlements. In the settlements a gathering of the heads of households determined who had to pay and how much. Since all were bound by a collective responsibility, by mutual surety, and there was no possibility of reducing the amount of the requisition, these gatherings were exceedingly noisy and sometimes even ended in blows: everyone wanted to pay as little as possible, but then his neighbour would have to pay more. They reckoned one another up to a nicety; for instance, if you had a dog, you would be told: 'You can feed a dog, so you can pay more than me'. And, seriously, the dogs in the countryside disappeared.

The cohort of those paying comprised 53 per cent of all farms in the *volost'*. But this does not mean that 47 per cent of the poorest did not pay. Frequently, a more prosperous man paid nothing at all, while a poorer but more timid one did. Their shouting often saved the 'bleaters' and the imposition fell on the less well-off and those who did not pay were the poor.

The requisitioning was not always fulfilled on time or completely. The *volost'* militiamen had continually to admonish and threaten the slackers. Our *volost'* paid almost all that was due from it, the shortfall was very small.

The decree of 21 April 1921 followed. In part it reads: 'The amount of tax shall be specified for each farm separately and calculated according to the amount of arable land and the number of consumers on the farm and the harvest in that locality'. Mutual responsibility was abandoned; this alone greatly loosened the bonds between people. Nevertheless, our *volost'* paid 15 categories of exaction (including labour and haulage obligations). Since the countryside had no clear conception of how much and just what had to be paid, the multiplicity of payments, sometimes in minute quantities (for example, 5 eggs per farm, a half or a third of a chicken), had an oppressive psychological effect on the payers: there seemed to be an endless chain of taxes of which you could never be free. It was no longer 53 per cent of all household heads in the *volost'* that were called on for payments in kind, as in 1920, but 87 per cent, hence a greater area of arable land was involved. Although in 1921 the whole *volost'* paid more tax in kind than in 1920, for the reasons just given, the rate per *desyatina* of arable land was lower. Poor farms, as long as they had some sown area, now also paid tax.

The tax was delivered to official procurement offices which were not subordinate to the Volost' Executive Committee, but dependent on the *uezd* and *guberniya*. The machinery for collecting tax in kind was extremely unwieldy. At the Tver' Guberniya Congress of Soviets in the autumn of 1921, in the course of a discussion, the question was raised as to what part of the tax was expended on organising its collection, storage and transport, etc. The pessimists asserted that the state would receive for its needs only

25 per cent of the total tax collected, the optimists said 75 per cent. I do not know who was right, but, in any event, even 25 per cent is not so little.

The same tax in kind was collected in 1922, but it was calculated in units of rye equivalent (according to a conversion table), thus the large number of varied exactions which had formerly existed disappeared. Everyone could pay the tax in the produce convenient to him (in accordance with the conversion table). I have estimated the tax only in units of rye. There was a reduction of 20 per cent for payment on time. Our *volost'* obtained this reduction, since it paid the tax in full and on time. A greater proportion of gross income had to be paid per unit of arable land than in 1921— Comrade Harvest had put us on the spot. Each head of a household hauled the tax 45 *verstas* to the *uezd* town.

The decree of 10 May 1923 established a unified agricultural tax in place of the tax in kind. The imposition of any kind of exactions on the farm additional to the new tax was made a criminal offence. The tax was assessed in rye units, but could be paid in money (or in units of the grain loan, which became widespread in our *volost'* in 1923). Despite an even lower harvest than last year's, this year the proportion of the gross harvest going to pay the tax was less than last year.

With this I shall end the present chapter.

Results

I have made a number of possible generalisations in the preceding exposition on the questions raised in the last chapters. In this chapter I shall try to evaluate in money terms all the economic benefits and losses to the population of the *volost'* I have studied throughout the revolutionary period. A number of following chapters, mostly as short as the preceding ones, will be devoted to brief sketches of the varied life of the Soviet countryside as I have seen it when investigating the economics of my own *volost'*.

In collecting and working on all the materials which I encountered in the course of my work I have tried, as far as possible, to be strictly objective and, in my opinion, have honestly taken account of all the profits and losses of the population in the *volost'* insofar as they could be taken into account and expressed in figures.

Out of caution I proceeded as follows, in order never to minimise the benefits to the peasantry in these years:

1. Official data I obtained from different sources (Guberniya and Uezd Statistical Offices, the Volost' Executive Committee), and cross-checked, show that in 1919 there was a failure to sow 36 per cent of the area. Unable to check this figure by personal observation, but knowing local conditions (a failure to sow 36 per cent is nonsense for 1919), I have counted only a 10 per cent failure to sow for 1919, basing myself on the figure for 1918, thus at once increasing the 1919 tilled area by 26 per cent; this, of course,

considerably reduces the burden of taxation on peasant land in 1919 (since the gross income from agriculture rose).

2. For 1920 (on the basis of my own observations) I excluded an area of 33 per cent not sown, which again led to a corresponding reduction in the burden of taxation on the land in 1920.

3. In dealing with the harvest yields we should use averages which are independent of chance phenomena (a harvest failure or an exceptionally good harvest). But I have used actual harvest yields and where, for the *volost'* in 1918 and 1919, these were close to the *uezd* average, I took these; since in 1920 and 1921 the yield for the *volost'* considerably exceeded the general average rate for the *uezd*, based on many years of observation, in all the estimates for 1920 and 1921 I allowed for the high yields; when, for the last two years, the yield fell, I took account of this fact too.

So what do the figures tell us? Has the present revolution so far been beneficial or, on the contrary, disadvantageous to my fellow locals in broad financial terms? I would remind you that I am writing of one *volost'*, not the whole country. Let us look at the table. The left-hand side shows the annual gains of the *volost'* population, the right-hand side, their losses. A careful reading of the notes to the table will make perfectly clear the derivation of all these figures, so I shall not explain them again.

In parallel with what I have said at the beginning of this chapter, I must stress that, without in the least wishing to minimise the benefits to the peasants over these years, I have, equally, not attempted to conceal the losses to the population in the same period, and thus:

1. I have estimated the losses from the lack of off-farm crafts and trades,

2. I have shown the losses to the population on deposits in the local loan and savings bank, and

3. I have (as far as possible) estimated the value of various exactions imposed on the population over all these years.

What do we get as a result of our book-keeping? Profit or loss?

Loss.

For the whole six-year period of 1918-23 I estimate this loss at:

611,219 rubles 45 kopeks (in pre-war money).

Or an average loss per year of

101,869 rubles 91 kopeks.

On average it amounts to 55 rubles 33 kopeks per peasant farm per year.

For one person it amounts to

11 rubles 24 kopeks per year.

So there is an undoubted loss. A loss proved, as they say, by hard figures.

But did this loss actually occur in real life?

I had to ask myself this question after I had totted up my figures. The point is that, having watched my *volost'* all those years and having it before my eyes all the time, I honestly cannot detect in actual daily peasant life the features of a gradual impoverishment extending from year to year. In the towns the ruin of the inhabitants, especially in the early stages of our revolution, hit one in the eye; townsmen were selling their 'movables and

TABLE 10

Profits and losses to the population for the whole revolutionary period

Gains	Rubles	Losses	Rubles
1918		*1918*	
1. The population did not pay the 12 per cent direct tax on gross income from arable land exacted from peasants before the revolution (1)	28,301·76	The population paid various in-kind and money taxes	12,199·22
2. The population did not pay indirect taxes, and here we count only the net government receipts from the sale of vodka (2)	24,306·48	The population lost deposits in the Goritsy loan and savings office (at the postal department) worth about 1 million rubles, or, in 1918 grain prices	2,854·00
3. The population did not pay for the school, maintaining the hospital and veterinary help and had free postal services (3)	20,623·68	The *volost'* population lost from off-farm crafts and trades which had ceased as a result of the revolution and the accompanying economic disorganisation of the country (4)	161,505·00
		Total	176,558·22
4. Benefits from the speeding up of house building (free materials for construction)	13,651·00		
Total	86,882·92		
1919		*1919*	
1. as 1 above	28,301·76	as 1 above	9,009·93
2. as 2 above (changed amount because of change in number of population)	22.904·64	as 3 above	161,505·00
3. as 3 above (changed amount because of change in number of population)	19,434·24	The population paid for items obtained at fixed prices	798·00
4. as 4 above (changed amount: although construction was faster than in peacetime, it was slower than in 1918)	7,410·00	Total	171,312·93
5. Benefits to the population from commodities obtained at fixed prices and by return payments for dues and taxes in kind	5,438·63		
Total	83,489·27		

Gains	Rubles	Losses		Rubles
1920		*1920*		
1. as 1 above (changed amount because of changed area of arable)	31,342·24	as 1 above		55,979.88
2. as 2 above	25,744·64	as 2 above		161,505·00
3. as 3 above	21,674·84	as 3 above		235·44
4. as 4 above	14,157·00		Total	217,720·32
5. as 5 above	4,160·98			
Total	97,079·70			
1921		*1921*		
1. as 1 above	31,342·24	as 1 above		60,919·47
2. as 2 above	23,493·36	as 2 above		161,505·00
3. as 3 above	19,933·76		Total	222,424·47
4. as 4 above	21,532·00			
5. as 5 above	6,510·99			
Total	102,812·35			
1922		*1922*		
1. as 1 above	31,342·24	as 1 above		37,419·00
2. as 2 above	23,007·60	as 2 above		161,505·00
			Total	198,954·00
3. as 3 above	19,521·60			
4. as 4 above	22,173·00			
Total	96,044·44			
1923		*1923*		
1. as 1 above	31,342·24	as 1 above		26,254·00
2. as 2 above	24,327·60	as 2 above (changed amount as off-farm crafts and trades again started to develop) (5)		160,321·88
			Total	186,575·88
3. as 3 above (postal services were now paid for, and not at a nominal rate as in 1922, so the benefit of free postal services is discounted for 1923)	18,337·85			
4. as 4 above	22,010·00			
Total	96,017·69			
Grand Total	562,326·37			
Loss 1918–23	611,219·45			
	1,173,545·82	Grand Total		1,173,545·82

Notes: (1) The following simple idea led me to consider as profits, both for 1918 and subsequent years, the direct taxes paid, as a percentage of the gross income of arable land, by the *volost'* before the revolution. While the *volost'* paid something as direct taxes in 1915, yet in 1918, after four hard years of a ruinous war, the *volost'* population still had in any event to pay a certain amount of direct taxes; it could not escape them entirely. Nevertheless, in 1918 the former 12 per cent of direct taxation was not exacted from the population; consequently, this money remained in their pockets (what was collected from them I have listed as losses), and was in this sense a profit. Indeed, this profit was actually or, more accurately, theoretically, greater than I have shown: had there been no revolution, the old regime was hardly likely to have continued to limit itself to 12 per cent.

(2) The population paid indirect taxes on tobacco, sugar and so on, but for the sake of simplicity, I have not calculated these taxes and so have not included them as profits. I have only taken vodka, the consumption of which in Tver' *guberniya* in 1913 was 0·66 *vedros* per person (irrespective of sex and age), i.e. amounted to 5 rubles 28 kopeks a year [*Statisticheskii Ezhegodnik po Tverskoi gubernii za 1913–14g.:113*]. I have assumed that the government pocketed 50 per cent of this as pure profit (in fact, it was much more).

(3) I have calculated as a very, very modest figure all the services the government supplied free to the population: schools, hospitals, veterinary points and postal services. I based myself on 1913 figures [*Ezhegodnik: 20 and 100–101, and Obzor Tverskoi gubernii za 1913 god: 31*], when the expenditure per person for our *uezd* was: education 0·94 rubles, medicine 1 r.; veterinary services 0·05 r.; postal communications 0·25 r., a total of 2r. 24k. During the past seven to ten years, however, the veterinary services have greatly developed; a medical centre has opened in the *volost'*, but ten years ago we did not have one; since 1918 medicine has made great strides: instead of one doctor we now have two working in the *volost'* hospital (in 1912 there were more than 14 thousand outpatients and over 8 thousand bed-days for inpatients; the corresponding 1918 figures are over 16 thousand and 9 thousand; for 1919 over 14 and 15 thousand; for 1920 over 19 and 17 thousand; the figures are taken from the hospital reports). Thus it is clear that the gain to the population under this item was in fact much higher than we have shown.

(4) How have I estimated the loss to the population of earnings from off-farm crafts and trades? I learnt from documents in the archive of the Goritsy post and telegraph department how much money the population received through the post in 1911, 1912 and 1913 (the three pre-war years) and took the arithmetic mean of that: 161,505 rubles. Obviously the population of the *volost'* (for example, carpenters who had worked in teams) brought home some earnings from off-farm crafts and trades in their pockets, not wasting money on postal transfers; but there is, of course, no way of allowing for such sums, but they could not have been very large. Overall, in pre-war Russia, crafts and trades brought each member of the rural population 12 rubles [*Larin, 1923:113*], but for our *volost'* it works out at about 24 rubles, so I have not minimised the losses compared with the average for Russia.

(5) In 1923 the population again began to receive money by post from those who had gone off to earn some money; the population received about 110,000 rubles by post. I have rejected this sum and recalculated it in grain prices.

immovables', down to the most essential items. We saw this at every step each day. Our *volost'*, however, has managed during the revolution to build itself up very, very much (see Table 11), but if there is impoverishment, no-one thinks of new buildings; the livestock situation is, if anything, somewhat better than in pre-revolutionary times; again, when the peasant is being ruined he takes the cow from the stall, not into it.

TABLE 11

Buildings in the volost'

	Total	of which, new:	
		peasant houses	*farm buildings*
1918	1,785	82	207
1920	1,836	84	222
1923	1,883	86	194

What has been happening, then? According to the figures there has been a loss, but on checking it turns out that somehow things are different!

The explanation is simple. I know perfectly well, because I have seen it for myself and because my fellow locals have frankly told me, that grain was sold at first (up to the autumn of 1922) at comparatively high prices (relative to the prices of urban output); when the price of grain fell, there was a mass development of home-distilling (cheap grain and potatoes are converted into an expensive product); then there was a widespread, destructive felling of timber for sale. All this gave, over the whole revolutionary period, a considerable revenue item. However, I do not know what figure to attach to this income: it is of a particular type which it is quite impossible to express numerically. This revenue, undoubtedly, offsets a considerable part of the deficit in the *volost'*, perhaps even covers it entirely. Thus, in conclusion, in summing up the entire revolutionary period so far, if we include items of income which it is impossible to allow for owing to special circumstances, the peasantry has not suffered financially from the revolution. I would add that, on the gains side, I have not taken account of the 8,482 *desyatinas* of land belonging to non-peasant private owners (we touched on this in the chapter on agriculture), which is partly now used by peasants (hayfields and a certain area of forest) and partly not (that included in the state fund). I have omitted this major source of gain because this entire stock of land is extremely fluid (whether held by peasants or the state), is constantly changing and no precise figures are available on it.

It goes without saying that the income derived from plundered forests, illegal home-distilling and speculative sales of agricultural produce cannot be considered as normal resources (I am making no moral judgment about this income) for the maintenance, still less for the development, of the peasant farm. That was why, at the end of the chapter on agriculture, I put forward certain thoughts about settling the question of the peasant farm. The time has now come, in my opinion, when the entire condition of peasant farming silently, but insistently, demands from the revolutionary government that the basis of and main relationships in the economic life of the village should undergo a revolutionary change. The countryside is wating . . .

In conclusion, I would stress that the following must be borne firmly and constantly in mind: in estimating the losses of the population in the *volost'* during the revolutionary period, I based myself on peacetime conditions; but between the 'good, old times' and the revolution there were years which were exceedingly hard on the economy, years of a burdensome war which ruined the country. These years, of course, crushed the economy of the countryside with their heavy tread; it is hard to believe anyone would challenge this. So my own *volost'*, too, crossing the threshold of the revolution, had behind it the dark shadow thrown by the war on its economy. That is why, taking into account what has just been said, it seems to me that the revolution has helped my fellow locals to rid themselves of the dark shadow of the imperialist war.

Commerce, Crafts and Trades

According to the latest map of the *guberniya* edited by G. T. Milov, head of the Statistics Office, Goritsy *volost'* is one of 35 trading districts of the *guberniya*. There was a fair in Goritsy eight times a year in peacetime; it had an annual turnover of one million rubles. At these bazaars, visiting

TABLE 12

Sales to volost' *population at fixed prices*

	Quantity (puds)	1919 Price (rubles)	Amount (rubles)	Quantity (puds)	1920 Price (rubles)	Amount (rubles)
Paraffin	—	—	—	138	2,400	331,200
Salt	345	400	138,000	716	800	572,800
Matches (boxes)	96,771	1	96,771	18,248	3	54,744
Shoeing nails	—	—	—	30	12,800	384,000
Tar	—	—	—	12	1,600	19,200
Spoons (number)	—	—	—	1,500	30	45,000
Textiles (arshins)	24,321	25	607,925	10,781	30	323,430
Sugar	172	600	103,200	—	—	—
Bricks (thousand)	72	200	14,400	78	8,000	624,000
Total			960,296			2,354,374

TABLE 13

Average Goritsy market prices (rubles/pud) and fixed prices for specified items

	1918 market prices	1919 market prices	1919 fixed prices	1920 market prices	1920 fixed	1921 market prices
Rye	350	2,400	53	10,000	70	90,000
Oats	105	1,350	50	8,500	55	30,000
Potatoes	60	350	45	5,500	50	8,000
Flax seed	—	—	90	17,000	150	120,000
Fibre	—	—	—	59,000	1,100	100,000
Beef	—	3,500	120	20,000	360	220,000
Russian butter	—	—	—	200,000	3,000	800,000
Wool, unscoured	—	—	—	100,000	3,600	—
Honey	—	—	—	200,000	3,000	800,000
Sheepskins, untanned (assumes 7 per pud)	—	—	—	42,000	358	—
Hay	—	600	15	6,000	60	15,000
Straw	—	—	3	1,500	15	6,000
Eggs (for ten)	—	—	—	2,000	33	—
Salt	—	28,000	400	48,000	800	200,000
Chicken (assumes 10 per pud, live wt.)	—	—	600	80,000	1,120	40,000
Paraffin	—	—	—	40,000	2,400	—
Sugar, granulated	—	32,000	25	160,000	—	—
Calico, medium quality (arshin)	—	300	—	3,500	30	—
Tar	—	—	—	20,000	1,600	300,000
Shoeing nails	—	—	—	80,000	12,800	200,000
Draught animals from Goritsy to Tver'	—	—	—	25,000	3,000	100,000
Draught animals from Goritsy to Korcheva	—	—	—	15,000	1,680	200,000
Draught animals from Goritsy to Podgorel'tsy	—	—	—	10,000	800	100,000
Draught animals for 10 versta journey	—	—	—	6,000	free	—
Work horse	2,500	60,000	—	400,000	—	—
Milch cow	700	20,000	—	250,000	—	—
Day rate for sawing timber	—	200	—	3,000	—	40,000

merchants bought up agricultural produce sent by the Goritsy population from the localities: up to 3,500 *puds* of rye and rye flour, 5,000 of oats, 5,000 of flax seed, 85,000 of flax fibre, 300 of linseed oil, 1,000 of butter, 500,000 eggs, 150 *puds* of ceps, 2,500 pairs of leather and felt footwear, 2,000 sheepskins, 100 wheels, 2,000 wood sledges, etc. As can be seen, the largest item in the bazaar trade was flax [*Statisticheskoe ekonomicheskoe obsledovanie gruntovykh dorog, vyp. VIII : 18*]. These products were supplied to the bazaars by the whole trading district centred on Goritsy, not by the *volost'* alone.

In Goritsy village there were fifteen shops, five or six pubs selling strong drink, a beer house and even the universal 'Singer Company'. There was also a shop of the Goritsy Consumer Society.

The Goritsy merchants were trading right up to the period of the 'nationalisation' of trade. As a result of nationalisation, we were left with two trading institutions: the pub 'from the Soviet', where travellers could get boiling water ('Soviet teas': carrots, chicory, etc. appeared later) and the consumer society shop, where the *volost'* population in 1919 and 1920 obtained various goods at fixed prices.

All that trading activity, which nevertheless took place in the *volost'* even at the time of the fiercest nationalisation, went, if one may apply the term, underground, i.e. became illegal.

They traded in grain and butter; these were the main items. These products were also hauled 75 *verstas* to Tver' and 45 *verstas* to Korcheva; in the *volost'* itself they also engaged in selling to the miserable, hungry townsmen who rode and came on foot in search of produce. The illegal trade was carried on in a military-style setting: ambushes were set up by members of the militia and the Red Army in various places in the *volost'*. If you were caught, they would seize everything. There were many abuses as a result of such 'seizures': produce was more often acquired by the members of the barrier detachments, and was only rarely delivered to the Executive Committee. A. Gurvich wrote about such detachments [*Izvestiya, 31 December 1918, No. 288*]: 'These detachments worked haphazardly, their activities were guided by the personal desires of their commanders. The overwhelming majority of these detachments were composed of the most unreliable and ignorant elements'. No-one subjected to this peculiar form of requisition, of course, dared complain about the abuses of the detachments, for fear of being hauled up for speculation. If abuses did come into the open, it was by chance. To carry from the *volost'* to Tver' a *pud* or two of rye, two or three measures of potatoes and ten pounds of butter was an exploit subsequently recounted with pride. Some bold spirits, undaunted by risky adventures or knowing how to 'smooth over' the commanders, made a packet in those days. But there were not many such. Other would-be speculators who exchanged their produce for the urban products essential to them paid quite dearly for those times. Nowadays, of a long winter's evening, many an interesting and tragic story is told of this heroic epoch.

To take our sole consumer society, until October 1922 it showed no activity or commercial initiative. Until the autumn of 1922 it was merely a distributor for the state; its employees were paid from the state coffers (6 men, their annual maintenance, in terms of grain, was 50 *puds*). The trade turnover of the society begins to rise from the end of 1922; 15 million rubles worth of goods (in 1922 paper money) were bought and 10 sold. In the first half of 1923, 900,00 rubles worth (in 1923 paper money) were received and 640,000 sold.

Apart from the consumer society, an agricultural co-operative society with more than 500 members had been organised in Goritsy in the autumn of 1921.

It should be noted, however, that as regards the population's commitment to the idea of co-operation, the activity of our co-operative societies has had little impact: you will not get members to meetings, they do not involve themselves, in private conversation they accuse the members of the board of self-interest, and so on. We lack people, both in the *volost'* and in the *uezd*, who could show the peasants the true, vital nature of co-operation.

When trusts began to appear in Russia, this innovation also came to us in Goritsy. At the end of 1922 and the beginning of 1923, four whole 'trusts' appeared in the village, springing up like mushrooms. There were, of course, no real trusts; they were the most ordinary rural shops, some belonging to a single person, some to a group, but all these little shops were fashionably called 'trusts'. Soon half of these 'trusts' went bust.

In any event, the New Economic Policy, proclaimed in Soviet Russia in the spring of 1921, began to develop in our *volost'* only in 1923 in the sense of the opening of shops, pubs, etc.

Postal statistics are of interest for a description of the legal trade. It is well known that advertisements, samples, prospectuses etc. are usually sent as printed matter; the *volost'* received the following printed matter:

1913	1,728
1918	1,092
1920	63
1922	—
1923	106

The trade centres have begun to feel out the *volost'* as an area for the sale of their goods and are sending us their advertisements announcing the resumption of some firm's 'former activity'.

The illegal trade in the *volost'*, however, did not die out with the proclamation of the New Economic Policy. In 1922, timber (beams, boards) and hooch were traded on the quiet, and they still are. Financially, these are very important items of trade. Thanks to hooch, for instance, many have got on their feet, as they put it.

As regards crafts and trades, as opposed to agriculture, three hamlets in the *volost'* which are on islands among the lakes engage in fishing as their basic occupation; nine hamlets engage in pasturing as an off-farm summer occupation. In peacetime the surplus element of the population scattered to the mills and factories of Moscow and Petrograd. Part of the basic male population usually went off to work as carpenters in neighbouring *volosts* in spring and autumn. There was also felt-making for felt footwear, tanners, etc. There was a windmill.

All these crafts and trades serving rural needs continue to exist now, at the beginning of 1924. Some of them, owing to circumstances, have become illegal of recent years; for example, at one time we were forbidden to tan sheepskins (I do not know why), but since the peasant has to have a sheep-skin jacket (demand creates supply), the tanning was carried on illegally.

The history of our mill, and of milling in general, is interesting. During the nationalisation of Goritsy 'industry and trade', the mill was also nation-alised. Its former owner continued to work at the mill as a 'specialist', and was paid a salary. Those bringing grain to the mill had to pay the treasury four pounds for every *pud* ground [*Sbornik dekretov i rasporyazhenii pravitel'stva po prodovol'stvennomu delu, kn. 4 : 258*]. Many peasants found it disadvantageous to grind their grain at the mill, and did it at home in a handmill (very hard work). Then, suddenly, everyone was asked to show their receipts for paying the milling due; war was declared on handmills. It turned out, according to the interpretation of the local authorities, that whether you ground your grain at the state mill or not, you still had to pay the four pounds of grain. Many paid, although many others dodged paying. From 1921 the mill was rented out (to its former owner), and three pounds per *pud* was charged for grinding (a saving for the *volost'* amounting, in 1921, for example, to more than 4,500 *puds*).

In the last two years the men of the *volost'* have started to go off elsewhere, but during 1923 some of those who had gone returned; they were on the point of establishing themselves when there were 'redundancies'. So back to the village.

That is how matters stand with commerce, crafts and trades.

The Grain Loan[2]

1922 . . .

Hardly any shares in the grain loan were distributed among the peasants of our *volost'*; only a few individual householders had them. There even existed a certain disbelief about the grain loan at the time of its first appearance.

They talked:

'What sort of a loan? . . . Grain! . . . There've never been loans like that before . . .'

'Our grain's now $4\frac{1}{2}$ million rubles a *pud,* and "they" say they buy a *pud* with shares, and at 3,800,000. You see, the clever boys have found their fools! . . .' 'They', of course, are the Communists. This term is met with both in the countryside and in the towns; passing the Field of Mars (now the Martyrs of the Revolution Field) in Petrograd by tram, a square made into one of the most beautiful in Europe in 1923, I often heard: 'Say what you like, "they" have done it well.' If you ask who 'they' are, the answer is 'The Communists, of course.'

'The Communists are smart, there's some sort of racket here . . .'

'It's an out-and-out swindle! . . .'

Autumn came. It was time to cart off the tax in kind. Those who had loan shares produced them instead of grain when delivering the tax in kind. The shares were accepted.

Then they began to say:

'They take them! They took them from Semen, he said so himself.'

'And they also took them from Ivan from Goritsy.'

'It looks as if we guessed wrong, old lads? Can't we put it right—rye's already 8 lemons (in the countryside millions are often called lemons) and we've still got to drag it 50 *verstas* through the mud to Kimry! . . .'

There were rumours that shares in the grain loan could still be bought in Tver' and Moscow. Smart chaps wishing to make a bit from reselling the shares set off for Tver' and Moscow. They came back soon and, in fact, brought a small number of shares which they straightaway sold in two or three days at a much-inflated price.

They were pestered:

'Are there any more?'

'No, that's all.'

'Why did you bring so few?'

They snapped back:

'So you think it was easy to get them? You should have seen the queues there. And I would have come back empty-handed, but luckily found an "acquaintance" in a bank clerk and picked up one or two. . . .'

Our consumer society had subscribed in good time for 500 *puds* in the loan. In December it got the grain, sold it and made a good profit on this deal.

'Well, they didn't guess wrong' the peasants said enviously of the 'co-op'.

1923 . . .

There had been a rumour since spring that this year there would be a grain loan. Our Tver' *guberniya* had been allocated to the third district, that with the highest share price of the loan. When the shares were still at 28 rubles each (in May 1923) they did not reach our *volost'*. They were sent in the beginning of June when the official price was then 40 rubles a *pud*.

Hearing that the shares had been sent, the peasants rushed to the village to buy them. Huge queues formed immediately. Only a few were satisfied.

I ask:

'Well, how was it; did you buy at 40?'

'Could you buy anything? Those nearest grabbed everything. The Soviet employees have made a packet. Some sharp lads took shares for about 60 to 80 *puds* and they don't need a fifth of that.'

'So you didn't get any?'

'Yes, I managed to get some. I had to pay 50 rubles instead of 40 and even then I scarcely made it, but I smoothed things over with a bottle of hooch . . .'

In one hamlet the executive committee chairman (N. S. Khorev) caught a swindler also selling the peasants a 'loan'. This lively lad had somehow got hold of an old receipt book of the Tver' branch of the State Bank somewhere and, taking the money, he filled in the amount and the number of *puds*: adding:

'When it's time to hand over the tax in kind, show my receipt.'

This swindle, of course, shows the popularity of the grain loan among my fellow-countrymen.

A little later they sent us an adequate supply of shares, and peasant demand for them was satisfied.

Four and a half thousand *puds* of the loan were sold in our *volost'* in 1923. But many, no doubt, bought shares outside the *volost'*, in Kimry, where our district usually makes its trade deals: sells its grain, butter, eggs, hooch, beams sawn up 'on the quiet' (which have been used for more than 300 buildings in Kimry), and so on. So it seems that the *volost'* has shares amounting to about 8,000 *puds* which cover about one third of the 1923 tax in kind.

Into whose hands in the *volost'* did the loan shares fall? This question can only be answered on the basis of personal observation, questioning, etc. My impression is that the shares fell into the hands of the most well-off peasants. The poorest peasants lacked the means to acquire them. If there is a third grain loan in 1924, it would be good to credit it to the weak peasants in the first place.

NOTES

1. The percentages supplied here from Bol'shakov's absolute figures show that this statement is not accurate.
2. The grain loan took the form of 'short-term bonds sold to the peasantry for cash, but valued in stable "grain units"—the government repaid cash purchases of bonds by cancelling the holders' obligations to pay the equivalent amount of tax in kind at the next harvest, or by repaying them in grain after the harvest.' [*Davies*, 1958:69].

The Journey of my Brother Alexei to the Land of Peasant Utopia

by

Ivan Kremnev

PART I

Foreword by P. Orlovskii

STATE PUBLISHING HOUSE, MOSCOW, 1920

Foreword

(From which the well-disposed reader will learn of the ideals of our co-operators and why these ideals are Utopian and reactionary).

The title of the book alone shows us that the author wants to transport us to a Utopian, i.e. non-existent, land, a land of fantasy, Many novels in this genre now exist in literature; they do not set out to depict that future social structure which should result from objective historical development, but rather try to represent those ideal conditions in which all the 'accursed problems', all the contradictions and injustices of a capitalist society, would be resolved. This Utopia, too, should be seen as another such attempt to resolve social questions. But since the author professes a particular class ideology, has his own social sympathies, his own social aspirations, then, of course, his whole Utopia, too, is tinged with these aspirations. That is not to say that he constructs his Utopia outside time and space; no, he takes his departure from contemporary Russia, and, with due regard to its class divisions, historically continues the development begun by the revolution of 1917. But, as an ideologist of the middle, the so-called 'working', peasantry, he rests all his hopes on this class, makes it play the decisive role in the future course of the revolution and direct the development of Russian society along the road of its class demands and aspirations. The historical moment depicted in *The Journey of Alexei Kremnev* is one when the peasantry, having reorganised everything in accordance with its demands, having realised its social ideal and achieved its own brand of 'socialism', has consolidated its power.

What, then, is this system with which peasant democracy rests content? In the social and economic sphere we find the complete domination of petty individual peasant producers on minute holdings of eight to eleven acres per household, but, thanks to high labour intensity, the productivity of the soil has been raised to almost three tons an acre. This is that same 'garden-bed cultivation' with the help of which the Demchinskiis[1] once attempted to preserve the peasant as a peasant, to attach him to the land, and to resist the revolutionising influence of the growing landlessness and proletarianisation of the peasantry. It was this intensive cultivation which for centuries made the Chinese peasant remain a slave to soil and toil, instead of becoming master of both so that he would serve man and aid his progress. For let us see what these three tons an acre mean. How are such harvests achieved? Primarily, of course, by a considerable increase in the weight of labour (its intensity); on this we have no quarrel with Kremnev: any society wishing to raise the material and spiritual level of the masses should begin by increasing labour intensity. But is the mere increase of labour intensity, *in a small production unit,* i.e. one essentially using manual labour, enough to achieve such productivity of the soil? Enough not merely to achieve yields of three tons an acre, but to continue raising them still further, for population growth is not arrested, and the quantity of land remains the same? Clearly, no. To achieve the required quantity of labour, the duration of work must also be extended. Unintensive labour cannot but be protracted. Given the very best conditions of sustenance, of life and of labour itself, there is a physiological limit to the quantity of energy which a man can produce in working. To exceed this limit machines must replace human labour, or the human body be destroyed by excessive extension of the work's duration. Only by such self-exploitation of the petty proprietor can the agricultural system of the land of Kremnev's Utopia be maintained. This complete enslavement of man by the soil is identical with that of the petty peasant proprietor we find in the West.

'Why the devil do you expend so much human labour on the fields? Surely your technology, which easily controls the weather, is capable of mechanising agricultural labour to free work hands for more skilled occupations?' asked Alexei Kremnev.

'That's it, there's our American talking!' Minin exclaimed. 'No, dear Mister Charlie, you won't get far against the law of diminishing returns. Our harvests of more than three tons an acre are achieved by practically looking after each ear of grain individually'.

We shall not pause here to consider how far the 'law of diminishing returns' is true, or whether such a law exists at all; we note only that, in so far as the phenomenon depends on natural conditions, it affects both large-scale and small-scale farms; and in so far as it is the result of mismanagement, of a plunderous exploitation of the soil, it can be eliminated equally well on the small- and the large-scale well-ordered farm that is not producing for the market and not under the pressure of market prices. The 'law' is, therefore, special pleading. But Minin and his ilk *need* this plea. The ideologists of the petty land-owning peasantry want to preserve the individual peasant farm at all costs. They know perfectly well that in its present form it will not serve as a foundation for the 'society of the future'. For to build such a society, with a high level of spiritual culture, a great deal of surplus labour is needed for public undertakings and institutions. Peasant labour today produces surpluses only under conditions of exceptional exploitation, or if the peasants do not eat enough; neither is acceptable in a land of 'Utopia'. What is the answer, then?

The solution is to hand: introduce mechanised work, collective farming, achieve this tremendous increase in output, not through the exhaustion and enslavement of men, but by means of technical improvement. Human labour, having become more intensive as a result of technical necessity, will then be reduced in quantity; man will be freed from the shackles of labour and will at last be able to enjoy the fruits of culture (for what use is culture unless it be accessible to each and every one?). That is what one might think . . . but then, you see, the petty individual independent working peasantry would disappear—and the main aim of our contemporary Minins is its preservation. Which is why they have to resort to methods that are truly 'Utopian'. The crops from the 'garden-beds' need to be increased ten-fold? That's nothing: we shall assume that in 'Utopia' the 'free' peasant's intensive labour produces three tons an acre instead of the former five hundred-weight . . . If the population doubles, crops of six tons can be attained. And so on. Quite clear and simple; but not convincing.

But let us continue. The peasantry has defeated the working class, but it has not destroyed industry, it has not even destroyed *private* industry. Admittedly, a considerable part of industry seems to be in the hands of co-operatives; however, all those enterprises where 'collective management is ineffective' or where 'the organising genius of high technology overcomes Draconian taxation' have remained capitalist in nature. Reflect on these reservations and you will see that the most powerful and technically advanced industries have remained capitalist. For it is precisely in those industries that the 'organising genius' has always performed miracles; and only they, in the face of competition, are able to overcome both Draconian taxation and all the labour legislation which, according to Minin, is more effective there than under the dictatorship of the proletariat. At the same time, the capitalist industry is supposed to act for the 'Comrade Co-operators' as that shark in the sea which, by its competition, prevents the co-operative fish from drowsing. All of which adds up to the most piquant aspect of the 'Peasant Utopia'; retention of an exchange economy and monetary circulation (see the newspapers where prices of objects for sale are quoted in grams of gold). This is very characteristic and proper: in a land of individual peasant farmers, the exchange economy, money, free trade with its consequent exploitation of labour, inequalities of wealth (this Minin himself admits), capitalism, and all the delights of the economic system just abolished in Russia are bound to survive. It is just that, officially, all this is preserved allegedly in the name of free enterprise, increased labour productivity and, of course, for the benefit of the ruling peasant class.

The peasantry as the dominant class is depicted very realistically in the Utopia; naturally, it could not exist without industry, but, at the same time, it is in its interest that the products of industry should be as cheap as possible. A numerous factory proletariat is essential to satisfy its enormous needs, but this class was defeated in the revolution; so the problem is resolved by delivering the workers into the hands of capitalists (private and co-operative) while protecting them by labour legislation. Like slaves, they are made to work for the peasant society; but to prevent the slaves rioting and again seizing power, they are safeguarded from excessive exploitation. That is what, by the laws of nature, the sensible thrifty little muzhik should do.

The peasants themselves, however, are not in evidence in the Utopia; a professional co-operator intelligentsia are the managers and rulers. And this fact brilliantly confirms Marx's words on the petty French peasantry in his 'The 18th Brumaire of Louis Bonaparte': 'They are unable to assert their class interests in their own name, whether through a parliament or through a congress. They cannot represent themselves, and must be represented. He who is to be their representative must also appear to them as their lord and master, he should appear before them as one holding authority over them, one wielding unrestricted government power, who will defend them against the other classes, and who will send them the rain, and the sunshine from above'.

In Ivan Kremnev's Utopia these words are substantiated with surprising accuracy. A small group of co-operator intellectuals rule the peasant state autocratically, deciding all affairs *for* peasants. Listen to Minin's language: 'We had to solve the problem of the individual and society. We had to build a human society in which the individual could feel completely un-fettered, while society would take care of the common interests by methods invisible to the individual'. No question of trying to master the laws of social development and, having learnt them, leading society by the most painless route towards its future—no, these people sit like high-priests in the quietude of their intellectual holy-of-holies, 'constructing human society' out of pure reason according to a preconceived formula. Is this not 'authority', is this not 'unlimited power', thinking and deciding for the class it represents? And this power does 'defend' its charges from other classes: it has neutralised the troublesome workers; it has imposed 'Draconian taxation' on the capitalists, it has introduced a 'Russian system' into the world economy whereby Russian grain is protected from the competition of technically superior countries, and the Russian peasant is enabled to regulate grain prices in accordance with the production costs of the small-scale peasant farm.* Finally, and this is comically characteristic, it send the peasants 'rain and fine weather'. As soon as the soil needs moisture, enormous magnetic stations are put into action inducing the required quantity of rainfall with the desired degree of accuracy. Exactly according to Marx! With such powers, the peasant has nothing to think of, nothing to worry about; he need only work, and in his spare time listen to Moscow's bellringing concerts.

The system which the author describes is the rule of an intellectual oligarchy endeavouring to satisfy the small peasants' class demands and able to achieve this only by creating an isolated economy in a closed system cut off from the world. It is the familiar organisation of large co-operative combines exalted to the rank of a social ideal and embellished with all those cultural and ideological accoutrements inseparable from any socialist utopia. This system is 'Utopian' in the everyday meaning of the word, i.e. lacking any real historical foundation, for it is entirely built on irreconcilable con-tradictions. To imagine that social equality and social justice can be preserved while preserving the individual farm, and, in industry, even capitalist production; to imagine that a peaceable working class happy with its slice of cake and its labour legislation, can exist side by side with massive and, with the Government's encouragement, continually growing tech-nological progress, and in a capitalist economy at that; to believe that on the ground prepared by world imperialism and by the workers' Internationale a separate closed 'Russian system', protected by a Chinese wall and rainshield, can be constructed—a system to which no general economic or social laws apply; to believe all this is to understand nothing of the laws of development of contemporary societies, to have learnt nothing from either capitalism or socialism.

Starting from primitive societies, mankind has been working towards the 'land of Utopia', i.e. towards a superior, socialist society, through a persistent, merciless class struggle for existence, for freedom, and for power. Each successful phase in the struggle has been marked by *technological achievement,* i.e. by an economy of labour, a reduction in the share of labour and an increase in the share of implements in the total productive forces; and every such successful stage has been the starting point for a further struggle in the same direction. Nor could it be otherwise. The liberation of man and of the human individual, raising him from the level of the work-ox to that of an intelligent, civilised sentient being, can only proceed hand in hand with his liberation from the curse of toil, from the need to give himself up entirely to heavy, mind-dulling physical labour. The apologia for labour as such was created by bourgeois ideologists, but in elevating labour into a virtue, they painted a picture of the labour *of others,* the labour of the proletariat. The labour which communism advocates rests on the conscious, intelligent will of the labourer, i.e. it presupposes his liberation from the enslaving labour of capitalist society. Thus, the reduction, the alleviation of labour, the replacement of man's labour by the work of machines, and in general the conversion of man from a slave of production to its master— this is the basic, essential, necessary premise for socialism.

In the land of peasant Utopia this condition is not met, at least, not in practice. The forms of the peasant economy which obtain demand not only highly intensive, but also exhaustingly prolonged labour, i.e. they are retrograde even compared with capitalist forms of agriculture where the working time is controlled by strikes and trade unions; this is why the Utopia is a reactionary one. Instead of man's thought moving forward in search of new ways and new forms, what has long been outlived is put forward as an ideal, decorated in fantastic colours and depicted as an attractive, happy future; and the reactionary nature of this whole social and economic system is shown clearly by the reactionary nature of its ideology. Minin, in fact, openly declares that there is nothing new in the 'peasant Utopia'. 'In fact, we had no need for any new principles; our task was to consolidate the old, centuries-old principles on which from time immemorial the peasant economy has been based'. And look at the glaringly characteristic details: the predominant style in the Minins' flat is strongly russified Babylonian. The national pastime is the game of knucklebones. Popular music is a bellringing concert (that means there are bells and churches and, consequently, there must also be priests working away to 'preserve the age-old principles'). In restaurants, the waiters wear white shirts and wide trousers, as floor waiters did in olden times; the peasant guard wears the uniform of Tsar Alexei Mikhailovich's musketeers, and so on.

To give the author his due, his descriptions of this reactionary ideology ring much truer than when he depicts the socialist beauties of the peasant Utopia. So we should be clear that the bells, the pub-waiters' white shirts, the knucklebones, etc. are an integral part of the picture of the state where the petty peasantry is the ruling class, but by no means the Botticelli paintings, the hundreds of frescoes or the parks on the ruins of towns. All the latter are inventions of the author, who, an art lover himself, tries to embellish the dullness of petty-bourgeois life in the land of Utopia—while the reactionary peasant ideology is the true reality. Take away these extraneous charms, and we are left with a country of heavy peasant toil on the 'garden-beds' of dwarf-sized plots, an enslaved factory proletariat, a cunning, scheming capitalist bourgeoisie able to evade all the 'Draconian' laws, and at the top the ruling 'co-operator' intelligentsia striving by any means to uphold this absurd system.

But perhaps it will be asked: if you are so opposed to this Utopia, why print and disseminate the book? This is why: this Utopia is a natural development, both unavoidable and interesting. Russia is a predominantly peasant country. In a revolution, the peasantry generally follows the proletariat, its politically more advanced and better organised fellow. The proletariat tries to lead the peasantry onwards to socialism, but this task demands much inner work in the peasant; and in the course of this internal regeneration, the peasantry will more than once, and for a long time to come, manifest its particular, narrowly peasant, and essentially reactionary ideals, will strive to cling to the past, to preserve the obsolescent, to restore what has gone, decorating it with scraps of socialist ideology. In the case of this struggle various theories of peasant socialism will arise, and various Utopias. What is printed below is one such Utopia. It has the advantage of being written by an educated, thoughtful man who, while embellishing his imagined future, like all Utopians, basically provides us with valuable material for the study of this ideology. He states sincerely what he believes and what he desires; and this gives his Utopia undoubted interest. We print it to enable all workers and, particularly, all peasants, who reflect seriously upon the great upheaval taking place in our lives, to understand how the future is conceived by people who think differently from us, and to form a critical and informed attitude to our opponents' arguments.

P. Orlovskii

NOTE

*Since the value of a product is determined by the quantity of socially necessary labour incorporated in it, doubling the quantity of grain harvested per acre as a result of doubling the quantity of labour (doubling the intensity) will not change the value of a unit of grain; whereas the same doubling of the product achieved by increased productivity of labour (the introduction of machines, etc.) at the same intensity, will *halve* the value of the grain. In a land of small-scale peasant production grain, naturally, will be dearer than in America, where wide use is made of machine production, and the whole 'Utopia' can only survive thanks to the artificial isolation of the 'Russian system'. Take away the barriers, and the whole system will collapse.

The Journey of my Brother Alexei to the Land of Peasant Utopia

PART I

THE APPEARANCE

Chapter 1

(In which the well-disposed reader becomes acquainted with the triumph of socialism and Alexei Kremnev, the hero of our story.)

It was long past midnight when the owner of labour book No. 37413, once, in the bourgeois world, called Alexei Vasil'evich Kremnev, left the stuffy, grossly overcrowded great auditorium of the Polytechnical Museum.

The misty haze of an autumn night blanketed the sleeping streets. The infrequent electric lights seemed lost in the far distance of intersecting alleyways. A wind stirred the yellowed leaves on the trees of the boulevard and in the gloom the walls of Kitaigorod loomed fabulously large and white.

Kremnev turned into Nicholas Street. In the misty haze it seemed to have taken on its former features. Wrapping himself up fruitlessly in his raincoat against the penetrating damp of the night, Kremnev looked nostalgically at the church of St. Vladimir and St. Panteleimon's chapel. He recalled how, when he was a first-year law student many years ago, with a faltering heart he bought Flerovskii's *ABC of the Social Sciences*[2] just here, on the right, from Nikolaev, the second-hand bookseller; how, three years later, he started his icon collection by finding a Novgorod Saviour at Elisei Silin's; and those many and long hours when, with the proselyte's burning eyes, he burrowed through the treasures of the manuscript and book stacks of Shibanov's secondhand shop, where now you could make out, under the dull light of a street lamp, the brief inscription 'Glavbum'.[3]

Banishing these guilty recollections, Alexei turned towards the Iberian Gate, went past the first House of the Soviets and plunged into the darkness of Moscow alleyways.

Words, phrases, and fragments of phrases just heard at the meeting in the Polytechnical Museum flashed morbidly through his mind:

'By destroying the family hearth we are dealing the final blow to the bourgeois system!'

'Our decree forbidding taking meals at home eliminates from our lives the joyful poison of the bourgeois family and firmly establishes the socialist principle for ever'.

'The cosiness of family life leads to possessiveness; the petty proprietor's joys conceal the seeds of capitalism'.

His tired head ached and was now, as usual, reasoning, but without conscious thought, and registering without drawing conclusions; and his legs mechanically moved towards the half-destroyed family hearth fated in a week's time to be destroyed completely in accordance with the decree of 27 October 1921, which had just been published and elucidated.

Chapter 2

(Telling of the influence of Herzen on the inflamed imagination of a Soviet official.)

Alexei buttered a large piece of bread, a blessed gift from the god-protected Sukharevka, poured himself a glass of boiling coffee and sat down in his working chair.[4]

The town could be seen through the panes of the large window; below, in the misty nocturnal haze, rows of street lamps stretched out in milky patches of light. Here and there, the dark bulks of houses, windows still alight, glowed a dull yellow.

'So, it's done.' Alexei thought, peering into the Moscow night. 'Old Morris, kind Thomas, Bellamy, Blatchford and you other good, dear Utopians.[5] Your solitary dreams are now common beliefs, your greatest. audacities have become an official programme and an everyday commonplace! In the fourth year of the revolution, socialism can consider it holds undivided sway over the globe. Are you satisfied, Utopian pioneers?'

And Kremnev looked at the portrait of Fourier hanging above one of his book-cases.

But for himself, old socialist, important Soviet worker in charge of a section of the World Economic Council that he was, there was something not altogether right about this realisation; there was a confused nostalgia for the past; some cobweb of bourgeois psychology still clouded his socialist consciousness.

He strolled up and down the carpet of his study, his glance sliding over the covers of the books; he suddenly noticed a row of small volumes on a half-forgotten shelf. The names of Chernyshevskii, Herzen and Plekhanov on the leather spines of the solid bindings caught his eye. Smiling a smile of childhood recognition, he took down Pavlenkov's edition of Herzen.

It was two o'clock. The clock struck with a long-drawn hiss and was silent once more.

Good, noble, childishly naïve words revealed themselves to Kremnev's eyes. He was engrossed and troubled by what he read as one is troubled by recollections of one's first youthful love, one's first youthful vow.

His mind seemed freed from the hypnosis of Soviet daily life; new, unhackneyed, thoughts stirred in his mind; he found it possible to think in new ways.

Excitedly, Kremnev read a prophetic page he had long forgotten:

'Weak, puny, stupid generations,' Herzen wrote, 'will somehow last until the eruption, until a flood of lava smothers them under a stony pall and confines them to the oblivion of history. And then? Then spring will come, young life will burgeon on their gravestones; the barbarism of infancy, full of unmatured but healthy strength, will replace the barbarism of senility, a wild, new power will burst forth in the youthful breast of the young nations; it will be the start of a new cycle of events and of the third volume of universal history.

Its basic tenor can be grasped now. It will be an era of social ideas. Socialism in all its aspects will grow to the utmost limits, to absurdity. Then again, a cry of refusal will break from the titanic breast of the revolutionary minority, and there will be once more a mortal struggle in which socialism, in the position of today's conservatism, will be defeated by another, unknown revolution still to come'.[6]

'A new rising. But where is it? And in the name of what ideals?' he wondered. 'Alas, it has always been the weakness of liberal doctrine that it was incapable of creating ideologies and had no Utopias'.

He smiled regretfully. 'O, you Milyukovs and Novgorodtsevs, Kuskovs and Makarovs, what Utopia will you paint on your banners?[7] What, save the obscurantism of capitalist reaction, have you to offer in place of socialism? I agree . . . ours is by no means a socialist paradise . . . But what will you give in its stead?'

The Herzen volume suddenly snapped itself shut with a crack; a bundle of loose octavo and folio sheets fell off a shelf.

Kremnev shuddered.

A suffocating odour of sulphur filled the room. The hands of the large wall clock spun faster and faster until they disappeared in a whirl. The pages of the tear-off calendar began to detach themselves noisily and spiralled upwards, filling the room with paper vortices. The walls became oddly distorted and trembled.

Kremnev's head swam and there was a cold sweat on his brow. He shuddered and in a panic of terror dashed for the dining-room door. It banged shut behind him with the crackle of breaking wood. He vainly felt for the electric light switch; it was not in its old place. Groping about in the darkness, he repeatedly struck unfamiliar objects. He felt dizzy and befuddled, as if he were sea-sick.

Exhausted by his efforts, Alexei lowered himself onto a sofa which had not been there before, and lost consciousness.

Chapter 3

(Depicting Kremnev's appearance in the land of Utopia and his pleasant conversation with a Utopian Moscow girl on the history of twentieth century painting.)

Kremnev was woken by a silvery bell.

'Hello, yes, it's me', a woman's voice was saying, 'Yes, he's arrived . . . evidently last night . . . still sleeping . . . He was very tired, fell asleep without undressing . . . Very well. I'll call you.'

The voice ceased and the rustling of skirts indicated that its owner had left the room.

Kremnev propped himself up on the sofa and rubbed his eyes in amazement.

He was in a large yellow room flooded by the morning sun. Its appointments were of a strange, unfamiliar style: furniture made of red wood with greenish-yellow upholstery, yellow curtains, half drawn over the windows, and a table with wonderful metal fittings. Light female steps were heard in the neighbouring room. A door creaked and there was silence once again.

Trying to understand his position, Kremnev leapt up and quickly walked up to the window.

Thick autumn clouds were sailing across the blue sky. A little below them, just above the earth, some small and large airplanes of bizarre design darted about, the revolving metal parts gleaming in the sun.

The town lay spread out below . . . undoubtedly, this was Moscow.

To the left, the bulk of the Kremlin towers reared up, on the right, the Sukharevka shone red, and, far off, Kadashi rose proudly against the sky.

A view he had known for many, many years.

Yet how much it had all changed! The piles of stone which had once crowded the horizon were gone; whole architectural complexes had disappeared; Nirenzei's house was no longer in its place . . . Instead, there were gardens everywhere . . . Sprawling clumps of trees enveloped the whole space almost up to the Kremlin itself, dotted with solitary islands of architectural complexes. Boulevards intersected the sea of greenery, now turning to yellow. Streams of pedestrians, motor cars and carriages poured along them in a living river. Everything breathed a certain distinctive freshness, a cheerful confidence.

Undoubtedly this was Moscow, but a new, transformed and brighter one.

'Have I really become the hero of a Utopian novel?' Kremnev exclaimed. 'A pretty stupid situation, I must say!'

He began to look around him to get his bearings, hoping to find some reference point that would enable him to identify the new world around him.

'What is waiting for me beyond these walls? The blessed kingdom of socialism, now consolidated and enlightened? The marvellous anarchy of Prince Kropotkin? Capitalism restored? Or perhaps some new, hitherto unknown social system?'

On the evidence of the view from the window, one thing was clear; people enjoyed quite a high standard of living and culture and lived in common. But this was not enough to understand the nature of his surroundings.

Alexei eagerly began to examine the objects around him, but they told him very little.

For the most part, they were articles of everyday life, notable only for the careful finish, a certain emphatic precision and luxury of execution and the peculiar style of their forms, reminiscent both of Russian antiquity and of the ornaments of Nineveh. A strongly russified Babylonian style, in a word.

Kremnev's attention was drawn to a large picture hanging over the heavily upholstered sofa on which he had woken up.

At first glance it might be confidently identified as a typical work of Pieter Brueghel the Elder. The same composition with its high horizon, the same bright jewel tints, the same foreshortened figures, but . . . the canvas represented people in coloured frock-coats, ladies with umbrellas and motor-cars, and the subject was undoubtedly something like the take-off of aeroplanes. Several reproductions lying on a neighbouring table were in similar style.

Kremnev went up to a large desk made from something like dense cork and hopefully began to look over the books that lay scattered there. These were the fifth volume of *The Practice of Socialism* by V. Sher, *The Renaissance of the Crinoline, a study of contemporary fashion,* two volumes of Ryazanov's *From Communism to Idealism,* the 38th edition of E. Kuskova's memoirs, a magnificent edition of the *Bronze Horseman,* a pamphlet *The Transformation of V-energy,*[8] . . . Finally, his hand trembling with excitement, he picked up a recent newspaper.

Impatiently, Kremnev spread out the small sheet. It was dated, 23·00 hours, 5 September 1984. He had leapt forward sixty years.

There was now no doubt that Kremnev had woken up in a land of the future; he plunged into reading the news-sheet.

'Peasantry', 'The past era of urban culture', 'State collectivism of sad memory' . . . 'This was in capitalist times, i.e. almost in pre-history . . .', 'The Anglo-French isolated system'—all these phrases and dozens of others penetrated Kremnev's brain, filling his mind with astonishment and a great desire to know.

The telephone interrupted his thoughts; steps were heard in the neighbouring room. The door opened and a young girl entered, together with a flood of sunlight.

'Ah, you are up . . .' she said gaily. 'I slept through your arrival yesterday.'

The telephone rang again.

'Excuse me, this should be my brother worrying about you . . . hello . . . yes, he is up now . . . I don't really know . . . I'll ask him at once . . . You speak Russian, Mister . . . Charlie . . . Mr Mann, unless I am mistaken.'

'But of course, of course,' Alexei surprised himself and exclaimed very loudly.

'He does—and with a Moscow accent . . . Alright . . . I'll hand you over.'

A confused Kremnev was handed something recalling an old-fashioned telephone set, heard a greeting offered in a soft bass, a promise to pick him up in three hours' time, and an assurance that his sister would take care of everything; putting down the receiver, he was aware very, very clearly that he was being taken for somebody else named Charlie Mann.

The girl had left the room. With the determination of despair Alexei rushed to the desk, hoping to find among the papers and bundles of telegrams some clue to the mystery surrounding him.

Luck was with him; the first letter he took up was signed by Charlie Mann who, in a few sentences, expressed his wish to visit Russia and become acquainted with its agricultural engineering installations.

Chapter 4

(Continuing the third and separated from it only in order to avoid excessively lengthy chapters.)

The door opened, and his young hostess came in carrying a tray with steaming breakfast cups above her head.

Alexei was enchanted by this Utopian woman, by her almost classical head, perfectly set on a strong neck, her broad shoulders and full breasts, which raised her shirt collar with every breath.

The momentary silence of first acquaintance soon gave way to lively conversation. Kremnev, avoiding the role of narrator, diverted the conversation into the area of art, assuming that this would not embarrass a girl who lived in rooms hung with fine examples of painting.

The girl, whose name was Paraskeva, spoke with the warm enthusiasm of youth about her favourite masters: Brueghel the Elder, Van Gogh, dear old Rybnikov and marvellous Ladonov. An impassioned admirer of neorealism, she sought in art for the secret of things, something either of god or the devil, but at all events beyond human capacities.

Recognising the supreme value of all that exists, she demanded of the artist a degree of harmony with the creator of the universe, prized the magic power in a picture, that Promethean spark which creates a new reality and all in all was closest to the realism of the Dutch Old Masters.

Kremnev gathered from her that after the era of the great revolution, when futurist painting was utterly disruptive of old traditions, there ensued a period of baroque futurism, of tame and charming futurism.

Then, as a reaction, like a sunny day after a storm, a thirst for craftsmanship came to the fore; the Bologna school came into fashion, the primitivists were somehow immediately forgotten, and hardly anybody visited the museum galleries containing the work of Memling, Fra Beato, Botticelli and Cranach. However, while losing nothing of its excellence, craftsmanship, with the passage of time, gradually acquired a decorative tendency and created monumental canvases and frescoes of the period of the Varvarin conspiracy; the period of still-lifes and the blue palette passed like a rage, then the twelfth-century Suzdal frescoes became the yardstick of the world's ideas and, finally, realism came to rule, with Pieter Brueghel as its idol.

Two hours had slipped by, and Alexei could not make up his mind whether he should listen to the deep contralto of his companion or watch the heavy plaits entwined on her head.

Her wide-open, attentive eyes and a mole on her neck spoke to him of the superiority of neorealism better than any arguments.

Chapter 5

(Excessively long, but essential to acquaint Kremnev with Moscow in 1984.)

'I'll take you through the whole town', Paraskeva's brother, Nikifor Alexeevich Minin, said, settling Kremnev in the car, 'and you shall see our present-day Moscow'.

They drove off.

The town seemed to be a continuous park amidst which architectural groups rose up to right and left, looking like lost little skittle pins.

Sometimes an unexpected turn of the avenue disclosed to Kremnev's eyes the outlines of familiar buildings, mostly erected in the seventeenth and eighteenth centuries.

Beyond the dense crowns of the yellowing maples, the domes of Barashi could be glimpsed; the limes fell back to disclose the magnificent silhouette of Rastrelli's building, Kremnev's school in his 'teens. In a word, they were driving along the Utopian Pokrovka.

'How many inhabitants are there in your Moscow?' Kremnev asked his companion.

'It's not so easy to answer that. If we consider the area of the town at the period of the great revolution and take the population constantly spending the night here, it now amounts to, perhaps 100,000 people; but forty years ago, immediately after the great decree on the destruction of towns, there were no more than 30,000. On the other hand, in daytime, if you reckon all the visitors and hotel guests, it might be over five million.'

The car slowed down. The avenue was narrowing; the architectural blocks approached one another closer and closer, old fashioned town streets began to appear. Thousands of cars and horse-drawn carriages, several abreast, sped along in a solid stream towards the town centre; a dense crowd of pedestrians filled the broad pavements. The almost complete absence of black was surprising: the bright blue, red, navy and yellow of the usually plain men's jackets and smocks mingled with the multi-coloured women's dresses, which were something like sarafans with crinolines, but in a great variety of styles.

Newsboys, flower sellers, peddlers of toddy and of cigars scurried about in the crowd. Over its heads and above the stream of vehicles, waving banners, with slogans and masts bedecked with flags, flashed in the sun.

Boys darted about, almost under the carriage wheels, selling some kind of news-sheet and crying for all they were worth: 'The decider! Vanya of Vologda against Ter-Markelyanets! Two jacks and one dog!'

There were lively arguments and exchanges in the crowd, and much was said about 'equalisers' and 'dogs'.

Kremnev raised his eyes in astonishment to his companion, who smiled and said:

'The national sport! Today is the last day of the international knuckle-bone championships. The Tiflis dibs champion is challenging the man from Vologda for the knuckle-bone championship. . . But Vanya won't go down, and this evening in Theatre Square he will be the winner for the fifth time.'

The car continued to slow down; it passed Lyubyanka Square, where both the Kitai-gorod wall and the Vitali cherubs had been preserved, and was going down past the First Printer.[9] A sea of heads, an explosion of bright flags flaming in the sun, a many-tiered platform rising nearly to the Bolshoi Theatre's roof, and the roars of the crowd filled Theatre Square. The knuckle-bone match was in full swing.

Kremnev looked to the left and his heart beat faster. The Metropole was not there. A formal garden had been laid out in its place, surrounding a huge column composed of gun barrels twined into a metal band spiralling upwards and decorated with a bas-relief. Atop the colossal pillar, three bronze giants stood back to back, holding one another's arm in a friendly gesture. Kremnev nearly cried out as he recognised their well-known features.

Without a doubt, on a thousand gun barrels, amicably supporting one another, stood Lenin, Kerenskii and Milyukov.[10]

The car turned sharply to the left and they passed close by the monument's plinth.

Kremnev had time to make out some of the figures on the bas-relief: Rykov, Konovalov and Prokopovich picturesquely grouped round an anvil; Sereda and Maslov engaged in sowing seed.[11] He could not hold back an exclamation of amazement. His companion replied through his teeth, without removing his smoking pipe: 'A memorial to the architects of the great revolution.'

'But listen, Minin, those people never in their lives formed such peaceful groups!'

'Well, to us, from a historical perspective, they were comrades in a single revolutionary effort, and, believe me, the present-day Muscovite doesn't remember very much what was the difference between them. Hey, blast it! Nearly hit that dog!'

The car swung to the left, the lady with the dog to the right; another turn, and the car dived into an underground tube, rushed along at a mad pace for some moments through a brightly lit subterranean tunnel, emerged on the banks of the Moskva and stopped by a terrace filled with tables.

'Let's have a *coca* and fruit-juice for the road.' Minin said, climbing out of the car.

Kremnev glanced around; before him rose the bulk of a bridge so exactly reproducing the seventeenth-century Stone Bridge that it seemed to have come from Picart's engraving.[12] Behind it, the Kremlin loomed in its full splendour, embraced on all sides by the golden autumn woods, its gold domes flaming.

A waiter in traditional white trousers and shirt brought them some drink resembling an egg-flip mixed with candied peel, and our travellers were lost in contemplative silence for a while.

'Forgive me,' Kremnev began after a time, 'but as a foreigner I don't understand the organisation of your town and I can't quite conceive the history of its dispersal.'

'Initially, Moscow's reconstruction was determined by political factors', replied his companion. 'In 1934, when power was firmly in the hands of the peasant parties, the Mitrofanov government, persuaded by many years' experience of the danger to a democratic regime from huge conglomerations of urban population, decided on a revolutionary measure. At the Congress of Soviets they carried through the decree which, of course, is also known to you in Washington, on the abolition of towns with more than 20,000 inhabitants.

'Obviously, the decree was hardest of all to carry out in Moscow, with its population of over four million in the thirties. But the leaders' obstinate determination and the technical capacity of the engineer corps were able to cope with the task in ten years.

The railway workshops and the goods yards were moved back to the line of the fifth ring road. The railway men of the twenty-two radial lines, with their families, were dispersed down the line no closer than that fifth zone, that is Ramenskoe, Kubinka, Klin and similar stations. The factories were gradually evacuated to new railway junctions throughout Russia.

By 1937 the Moscow streets began to empty. After Varvarin's conspiracy, the work naturally intensified; the engineer corps set about planning the new Moscow; the city's skyscrapers were destroyed by the hundred; dynamite had often to be used. My father recalls that in 1939 the boldest of our leaders, wandering through the ruins of the town, were ready to acknowledge themselves vandals, Moscow was such a picture of devastation. But the destroyers had before them Zheltovskii's plans and the work continued stubbornly.[13] To reassure the population and European opinion, one sector was completely finished in 1940; that astonished them and calmed feelings; and by 1944 everything came to look as it does now.'

Minin took from his pocket a small plan of the town and spread it out.

'But now the peasant regime has grown so strong that this decree we regard as sacred is no longer observed with the former puritanical severity. Moscow's population is growing so much that, in order to observe the letter of the law, our councillors count as Moscow only the ancient White Town, that is the area within the perimeter of the pre-revolutionary boulevards.'

Kremnev carefully examined the map, then looked up.

'Excuse me,' he said, 'but this is some kind of sophistry; all this, around the White Town, that's almost a town. And, altogether, I don't see how you could have agrarianised the country painlessly and what possible part your pathetic pigmy-towns could play in the economy.'

'I can't easily answer your question in a couple of words. You see, formerly the town was self-sufficient, the countryside was no more than its hinterland. Now, if you like, there are no towns at all, there are only nodal points of the nexus of social relations. Each of our towns is simply an assembly point, the central area of an *uezd*. It's not a place for living, but a place for celebrations, gatherings and some other matters. A point, but not a social entity.'

Minin raised his glass, drained it at a gulp and continued.

'Take Moscow: with its 100,000 population, it has hotels for four millions; the *uezd* towns, with populations of 10,000, have hotels for 100,000, and they are hardly ever empty. Communications are such that every peasant can reach his town in an hour and a half, and visits it frequently.

But it's time we were on our way. We have to make a pretty big detour and pick up Katerina at Arkhangel'skoe'.

The car set off again, turning towards the Prechistenskii Boulevard. Kremnev looked round with surprise; instead of the golden church of Christ the Saviour, shining like a Tula samovar, he caught sight of gigantic ruins, ivy-covered and evidently carefully preserved.

Chapter 6

(In which the reader will conclude that after 80 years they have not forgotten in Arkhangel'skoe how to make vanilla cheese-cake for tea.)

The old statue of Pushkin stood out among the spreading limes of the Tver' Boulevard.

Erected on the spot where Napoleon had once hanged those alleged to have set fire to Moscow, the monument had been a silent witness to the fearful events of Russia's history.

Pushkin in effigy had seen the barricades of 1905, the nocturnal meetings and Bolshevik guns of 1917, the trenches of the peasant guard of 1932 and Varvarin's mortars of 1937; and there he still stood, still placidly contemplative, awaiting further developments.

Once, and only once, had he tried to intervene in the elemental turmoil of political passions, when he reminded the crowd at his feet of his tale of the fisherman and the fish. But they had not listened . . .

The car turned into the Grand Avenues to the west. The quiet and dusty Tver' and Post-horse Streets had once stretched here. Their monotonous series of buildings had been replaced by the luxuriant limes of

the Western Park, and only the domes of the cathedral and the white walls of
the Shanyavskii University rose from the thickets, like islands amidst the
waving green sea.[14]

Thousands of cars glided over the asphalt of the great West road. Newsboys and flower sellers dashed about the avenues, dotted with the yellow
awnings of cafes and alive with a motley crowd; hundreds of aerocutters
were so many small and large black specks against the immobile clouds,
while heavy passenger airflyers took off from the Western Aerodrome.

The car sped past the avenues of Petrovskii Park filled with the noise of
children's voices, slid by the hothouses of the Silver Wood, turned sharply
left and darted like an arrow down the Zvenigorod Highway.

They still did not seem to be out of the town. The same fine avenues
extended to right and left, they glimpsed many white two-storey houses
and sometimes whole architectural groups, only instead of flowers between
the rows of mulberry and apple trees, there would be strips of vegetable
gardens, rich pastures and strips of harvested corn.

'Well,' Kremnev turned to his companion, 'your decree on the abolition
of urban settlements has evidently been observed only on paper. The Moscow
suburbs have stretched far beyond All Saints'.

'I am sorry, Mister Charlie, but we are no longer in the town, this is
typical north Russian countryside.' And he explained to the astonished
Kremnev that the density of peasant population in the Moscow *guberniya*
had become so high that the countryside had taken on an aspect unusual
for rural settlements. 'Now the whole area for hundreds of miles around
Moscow is a continuous agricultural settlement, intersected by rectangles
of common forest, strips of co-operative pastures and huge climatic parks.

In areas of farmstead settlement, where the family allotment is no more
than 8-10 acres, you will find peasant houses almost side by side for dozens
of miles. They are only screened from one another by closely planted rows
of mulberries or fruit-trees, which have now become common. Actually, it
is time to give up the old-fashioned division between town and country,
because all we have is a more or less dense distribution of the same agricultural population.'

'You see those groups of buildings,' Minin pointed far to the left, 'that
stand out a little because of their size? They are the "townships" as they are
now usually called. The local school, a library, a hall for entertainments
and dances, and other community facilities. A small social centre. Today's
towns are just the same social centres of the same rural life, only bigger.
And now we have arrived.'

The forest opened out to reveal, in the distance, the graceful silhouette
of the Arkhangel'skoe palace.

The car made a sharp turn and, rumbling over the gravelled drive,
passed under the wide gate crowned with a trumpeting archangel to pull
up by the orangery wing, scattering as it did so a whole flock of young
girls who had been playing hoop-la.

White, pink and blue dresses surrounded the newcomers and a girl of about seventeen threw herself with a cry of joy into the arms of Alexei's companion.

'This is Mister Charlie Mann. My sister, Katerina'.

A moment later the guests were seated on the lawn of Arkhangel'skoe park, amongst statuary busts of ancient philosophers, by a purring samovar set on a table; on the linen tablecloth, mountains of rosy cheese-cakes were piled up.

Alexei was gorged with the cakes, seductive, rich, vanilla cheese-cakes, with fragrant tea; he was bestrewn with flowers and questions on American morals and customs and whether they knew how to write poetry in America. Afraid of getting caught out, he counter-attacked, asking them two questions for every one that was put to him.

Tucking into cheese-cake after cheese-cake, he learnt that Arkhangel'skoe belonged to the Brotherhood of Saints Flor and Lavr, a kind of lay monastic order, whose numbers were recruited from talented young boys and girls excelling in the arts and sciences.

Down the suites of the old palace rooms and the lime-tree avenues of the park, once celebrated for Pushkin's visits and the brilliant, gallant life of Boris Nikolaevich Yusupov, with his Voltaireianism and his colossal library devoted to the French revolution and gastronomy, there now echoed the voices of this young band of bearers of Prometheus' creative flame, sharing life's labours and joys.

The Brotherhood had a couple of dozen magnificent, huge estates scattered over Russia and Asia, equipped with libraries, laboratories, picture galleries, and represented as far as could be seen one of the most powerful creative forces in the land. Alexei was astounded by the strictness of the almost monastic rule and the radiant, ringing joy which permeated all around; the trees, the statues, their hosts' faces and even the threads of the autumn cobwebs floating in the sun.

But all this was insignificant compared with the piercing eyes and melodious voice of Paraskeva's sister. Alexei was positively crazy about Utopian women.

Chapter 7

(Convincing those so inclined that the family is the family, and ever shall be.)

'Hurry, my friends, hurry', Minin urged his passengers, stacking Katerina's bundles and bags in the car, 'a general rain is due to start at 9 o'clock today and the meteorophores will be raising tornadoes in an hour'.

Although this tirade should have prompted Kremnev to surprise and interrogation, it did not do so, since he was wholly absorbed by the process of wrapping up Paraskeva's sister in scarves.

When, however, the car was noiselessly gliding along the New Jerusalem Chausee, and fields, with thousands of peasants working hurriedly to gather in the last stacks of oats, flashed by on both sides, he could restrain himself no longer and asked his companions:

'Why the devil do you expend so much human labour on the fields? Surely your technology, which easily controls the weather, is capable of mechanising agricultural labour to free work hands for more skilled occupations?'

'That's it, there's your American talking!' Minin exclaimed. 'No, dear Mister Charlie, you won't get far against the law of diminishing returns. Our harvests of more than three tons an acre are achieved by practically looking after each ear of grain individually. Agriculture has never been as manual as now. And at our population densities, this is no fad, but sheer necessity. That's why!'

He fell silent and increased the speed. The wind whistled past and Katerina's scarves fluttered over the car. Alexei watched her eyelashes, the lips glimpsed through folds of the scarf and felt he had known her since time began . . . A tender smile filled his heart with joy and comfort.

It was growing dark, and clouds had piled up in the sky, when the car approached the little houses on the steep banks of the Lama.

The extensive Minin family occupied several little houses built in the simple style of the sixteenth century; the surrounding palisade gave the estate the aspect of a small, ancient town. The barking of dogs and the hum of voices met them as they drove up to the gates. Some hefty lad seized Katerina in his arms, two little girls and a boy flung themselves on the parcels of provisions from Moscow, a girl in her teens was demanding some letter, and a grey-haired old man, who turned out to be Alexei Alexandrovich Minin, the head of the clan, took his namesake under his care and went to allocate him his room, wondering at the purity of his speech and the cut of his American clothes which vividly reminded him of the fashions of his distant childhood.

In about ten minutes, washed and combed, and feeling entirely confused, Alexei entered the dining room. At the flower-covered table a lively argument was in progress, and he had barely crossed the threshold when he was immediately chosen to arbitrate as a 'completely impartial' person. Two flat dishes were submitted to his expert judgment: one decorated with crayfish and black grapes, the other bearing a composition of a lemon, red grapes, and a cut glass goblet of wine. The two contenders, Meg and Natasha, demanded in the ringing tones of their fifteen-year-old voices a decision on whose still-life was 'more Dutch'.

Not without difficulty, Alexei solved his predicament by identifying one composition as an unrecognised authentic Jacob Pooter and the other a copy after Willem Kolff, and was rewarded with applause and a huge slice of cream cake, invented, as he was informed, by the professor of cookery herself, the absent Paraskeva.

Little Antoshka tried to learn from the American whether it were true

that sperm whales could be caught with hook and line in Hudson Bay, but
was immediately despatched to bed. An elderly lady pouring herself a third
glass of tea, inquired whether Alexei had children and marvelled that his
wife had allowed him to fly across the Atlantic. Much abashed by Alexei's
assurance of the absence of any signs of spouse, she was preparing to continue the investigation, but at that point someone's hands tied a scarf over
his eyes and he realised, or rather felt, that Katerina was standing behind
him.

'Blindman's buff, blindman's buff', called the children, dragging him into
the hall, and he was obliged to do a lot of chasing before he caught Katerina
in his arms.

Alexei Minin appeared to restore order and, freeing Kremnev from his
captivity, set him by the fireplace and spoke as follows:

'Tonight, when you are straight from your journey, I should not like to
burden you with business talk. But all the same, tell me, what is an isolated
American's first impression of our native land?'

Kremnev launched into assurances of his surprise and delight, but the
strains of a harpsichord terminated their conversation. Katerina had roped
in her brother as accompanist and was singing Alexandrov's romance to
Derzhavin's words:

> Golden sterlet from the Sheksna,
> Cream and borshch wait our desire
> Wine and punch in the decanter
> Tempt with sparks of ice and fire.

There followed 'The Peacock', and the duet 'The young couple's new
home', and Kremnev felt she was singing for him, that she did not want
him to attend to anyone else.

The 'general' rain due from 9 till 2 in the morning was pouring down
outside in dense streams. The room became even cosier, the peace of the
family contentment was warmed by the dying fire. Aunt Vasilisa was telling
Natasha's fortune from the cards; the young people were planning how best
to show the American round Yaropolets and White Kolp'. However, Alexei
Minin categorically announced that he had bespoken Mister Charlie for
the whole morning and that it was time for all to go to bed.

Kremnev asked Meg for her textbook on world history to read before
going to sleep and, accompanied by Katerina and the hellish rain, made his
way to the wing allotted as his quarters.

Chapter 8

(Historical)

Katerina made Kremnev's bed, and putting some gingerbread biscuits and
dates on the table, looked at him fixedly and suddenly asked:

'Are they all like you in America?'

Alexei was dumbfounded, and the equally confused young lady ran off, banging the door; through the steamed up window panes the retreating light of her lamp flickered away.

Kremnev was alone.

It took him a long time to recover from the impressions of that extraordinary day, all the marvels of which were nevertheless surpassed by the bewitching form of Paraskeva's sister.

Pulling himself together, Kremnev undressed and opened the history textbook.

At first he could understand nothing; it expounded at length the history of Yaropol'e *volost'*, then the history of Volokolamsk, and that of the Moscow *guberniya*, and only the final pages of the book dealt with the history of Russia and the world.

With mounting excitement, Kremnev swallowed page after page, gobbling up historical events together with Katerina's gingerbreads.

Coming to the events of his own era, Kremnev learnt that the world unity of the socialist system did not last long; the prevailing concord was very quickly disrupted by centrifugal social forces. No socialist dogma could expunge the ideas of military revenge from the German soul, and over the trifling matter of sharing out the Saar coal, the German trade unions compelled Radek, their president, to mobilise the metal workers and coal miners and occupy the Saar basin by armed force until the problem could be solved by the Congress of the World Economic Council.[15]

Europe again broke down into its elements. The structure of world unity collapsed and a new, bloody war started, during which in France the aged Hervé succeeded in carrying out a social revolution and establishing an oligarchy of senior officials of the Soviets.[16] After six months of bloodshed, peace was restored by the joint efforts of America and the Scandinavian Union, but at the price of dividing the world into five closed economic systems—German, Anglo-French, American-Australian, Japan-China and Russian. Each of these isolated systems was allocated pieces of territory in all climatic zones, sufficient to ensure their economic existence, and thereafter, while preserving a community of culture, they developed altogether different political and economic ways of life.

In Anglo-France the oligarchy of Soviet bureaucrats degenerated very quickly into a capitalist system. America returned to parliamentarianism and partly denationalised its production, though basically maintaining its state-run agriculture. Politically, Sino-Japan rapidly reverted to monarchism, but preserved peculiar forms of socialism in the economy. Only Germany continued the regime of the 1920s totally uncorrupted.

The history of Russia was as follows. While the system of Soviets was piously maintained, it was found impossible to complete the nationalisation of agriculture.

The peasantry, representing a massive social force, proved hard to communise, and within five or six years of the end of the civil war, peasant groups began to exert an impressive influence both in the local soviets and also in the All-Russia Central Executive Committee.

Their strength was considerably weakened by the policy of appeasement of the five Socialist Revolutionary parties, which frequently undermined the influence of purely class-based peasant associations.

For ten years no single tendency had a stable majority at the Congresses of Soviets; in practice, power belonged to the two communist factions, always able at moments of crisis to come to an arrangement and bring masses of workers out into the streets in impressive demonstrations.

But the conflict which arose between them over the decree on the compulsory introduction of eugenics created a situation from which the rightwing communists emerged victorious, but at the price of forming a coalition government and changing the constitution to give parity of voting power to peasants and townsmen. The re-elected soviets produced a new Congress of Soviets with an absolute preponderance of purely class-based peasant groupings, and from 1932 there had been a permanent peasant majority in the All-Russia Central Executive Committee and at congresses, and the system had been slowly evolving towards an increasingly peasant regime.

However, the dualist policy of the socialist revolutionary intelligentsia and the tactics of street demonstrations and uprisings had more than once shaken the foundations of the Soviet constitution, obliging the peasant leaders to retain the coalition formula in the composition of the Council of People's Commissars; a procedure encouraged by the numerous attempts at a reactionary coup by certain urban groups. In 1934, after a rising aimed at establishing an intellectual oligarchy on the French model, and supported for tactical reasons by the metal and textile workers, Mitrofanov organised the first purely peasant-class Council of People's Commissars and at the Congress of Soviets carried through the decree on the destructions of towns.

Varvarin's rising of 1937 was the last manifestation of the political role of the towns before they dissolved in the sea of peasantry.

The General Land Plan was adopted and implemented in the 1940s; the meteorophores, a network of magnetic power stations, using A. A. Minin's method for controlling the weather, were set up. The sixties were marked by violent religious disturbances and an attempt by the Church to seize lay power in Rostov district. His eyelids were drooping and his exhausted brain could take no more.

Kremnev put the light out and closed his eyes. But Katerina haunted him for a long time, and it was late into the night before he fell asleep.

Chapter 9

(Which young lady readers may skip, but which is recommended for the particular attention of members of the Communist Party.)

The sole embellishments of Alexei Alexandrevich Minin's ample study were bookshelves gleaming with the dull gilt of leather bindings and a few Vladimir-Suzdal' icons.

A portrait of his father, a well-known professor in Voronezh and later in Constantinople, completed the room's appointments in deep indigo tones throughout.

'I must acquaint you', his hospitable host began, 'with the realities of life in these parts, for without such knowledge you will not be able to understand the significance of our engineering installations or the very possibility of their existence. But, Mister Charlie, I really am at a loss where to begin. You are, as it were, a visitor from the other world, and it is difficult for me to judge what aspect of our life is particularly new and unexpected to you'.

'I should like to learn', Kremnev said, 'about the new social principles on which Russian life was built after the peasant revolution of the thirties; without these, I think, it would be difficult to understand all the rest'.

His companion was slow to answer, as if considering how to tell his story.

'You want to know about those new principles', he began, 'which peasant power introduced into our social and economic life. In fact, we had no need of any *new* principles; our task was to consolidate the *old*, centuries-old, principles on which from time immemorial the peasant economy had been based.

Our only aim was to assert these great ancient principles, to enhance their cultural value, to transform them spiritually and to endow their embodiment with a social and technical organisation which would enable them not only to display that peculiarly passive resilience which has characterised them for ages, but also to have active strength, elasticity and, if you like, striking power.

Our economic system, like that of ancient Rus', is founded on the individual peasant farm. We considered it, and still do so, the ideal model of economic activity. In it, man confronts nature; in it, labour comes into creative contact with all the forces of the cosmos to produce new forms of existence. Every workman is a creator, each manifestation of his individuality represents the art of work.

I need not tell you that living and working conditions in the countryside are the healthiest, that the peasant farmer's life has the most variety etc., or any of the other self-evident facts. This is man's natural condition, from which he was exiled by the demon of capitalism.

However, in order to establish a twentieth-century nation on the basis of the peasant farm and the peasant way of life, it was essential for us to solve two basic organisational problems.

The *economic* problem was to create a national economic system which would be based on the peasant farm and retain its leading role, and also economic machinery which in its functioning would not be technically inferior to any other conceivable mechanism and would sustain itself automatically without recourse to state compulsion of a non-economic nature.

The *social,* or, if you like, the cultural problem, was how to organise the social existence of the broad masses so as to preserve, in conditions of scattered rural settlement, the highest forms of culture, which had long been the monopoly of urban civilisation, and to ensure that cultural progress in all spheres of mental and spiritual life would be at least equal to that under any other regime.

And mark, Mister Charlie, that we not only had to solve both these problems, but also had to think deeply about the means for solving them. For us not only *what* we wanted to achieve was important, but also *how* it might be achieved.

The period of state collectivism, when ideologists of the working class were realising their ideals on earth by the methods of enlightened absolutism, had brought Russian society into such a condition of anarchic reaction that no new regime could be introduced by edict or decree sanctioned by the force of the bayonet.

Besides, any idea of a monopoly in the sphere of social creation was alien to the very spirit of our ideologists.

Our leaders, who were not proponents of a monist outlook, thought or action, had, for the most part, a mentality capable of accommodating a pluralistic view of the world, and so believed that life is worthwhile when it permits the full realisation of all the possibilities, all the new departures, contained in it.

In brief, we had to resolve these problems in such a way as to leave to any initiative, any creative effort, the chance of competing with us. We endeavoured to conquer the world by the inner strength of our cause and our organisation, by the technical superiority of our organising principle, not by smashing in the face of anyone who thought otherwise.

Apart from that, we have always recognised that the State and its apparatus are by no means the sole manifestation of social life, and so, in our reforms, we have for the most part relied on social methods of solving problems, not measures of state coercion.

Still, we were never blindly addicted to principle; and when outside violence threatened our cause, and expediency made us remember that state power was in our hands, our machine guns worked no worse than those of the Bolsheviks.

Of the two problems I have outlined, the economic one presented us with no particular difficulties.

You know, of course, that in the socialist period of history the peasant farm was considered as something inferior, as that proto-matter from which the 'higher forms of large-scale collective economy' should crystallise out. Hence the old idea of grain and meat factories. It is now clear to us that this view has not so much a logical, as a genetic origin. Socialism was conceived as the antithesis of capitalism; born in the dungeons of the German capitalist factories, nurtured in the minds of an urban proletariat haunted by forced labour, by generations that had lost the habit of any individual creative work or thought, it could conceive of an ideal system only as the negation of the system it knew.

Hirelings themselves, the workers, in constructing their ideology, made servitude an article of faith of the future system, and created an economy in which all were performers and only a few individuals possessed the right to creative activity.

But forgive me, Mister Charlie, I digress. Well then, the socialists conceived of the peasantry as proto-matter, since they had economic experience only in the field of manufacturing industries and could reason only in terms of their own organic experience.

But to us it was perfectly clear that, in social terms, industrial capitalism was merely a pathological, monstrous condition by which manufacturing industry, owing to its pecularities, had been affected, and by no means a developmental stage of the economy as a whole.

Thanks to its fundamentally healthy nature, agriculture had avoided the bitter cup of capitalism and we had no need to direct our developmental process into that channel. Particularly, since the German socialists' collectivist ideal itself, in which the working masses were conceived as the executors of agricultural work in accordance with State directives, seemed to us socially very imperfect compared with a system of working peasant farmers, a system in which labour is not separated from creative management, in which the freedom of individual initiative allows each human being to develop his full spiritual potential, while enabling him also when necessary to make use of the whole might of the collective large-scale economy and of public and state organisations.

Already at the beginning of the twentieth century the peasants had collectivised and organised in large co-operative enterprises all those branches of their productive activity where big economic units scored over small ones; in its present form this gives us a very stable and technically advanced structure.

This is the buttress of our economy. It was much more difficult to deal with the manufacturing industries. There it would have been foolish, of course, to expect to restore family production.

For most sectors, artisan activity and cottage industry were out of the question in the overall majority of branches of production, given the present level of factory techniques. But here, too, peasant initiative got us out of our difficulties; peasant co-operatives with their guaranteed and very large market, nipped in the bud any chance of competition for most products.

Admittedly, we aided them a little in this, by breaking the backs of capitalist factories with swingeing taxation which was not applied to co-operative enterprises.

However, we still have private initiative of capitalist type; in those areas where collectively managed enterprises are ineffective, and in those cases where an organising genius can overcome, thanks to advanced technology, the effects of our Draconian taxation. We don't even try to kill it, for we consider it essential to preserve for our comrade co-operators a degree of threat from permanent competition, and thus save them from technical stagnation. We know that our present-day capitalists, too, have certain shark-like propensities, but then we all know that there are sharks in the sea so that the other fish should not doze.

But this residual capitalism is very tame and so, indeed, is the co-operative industry, though more inclined to rebel, for our labour laws protect the worker from exploitation even better than the laws of the dictatorship of the proletariat under which a colossal share of surplus value was absorbed by the herds of officials in the Chief Administrations and the Administrative Centres.

Well, apart from that, we got rid of all the economic enterprises, only keeping for the State monopolies in forestry, petroleum and coal; for having control of fuel, we control the whole of manufacturing industry.

If I add, that our trade is predominantly in the hands of co-operatives and that state finance is based on the taxation of profits of enterprises employing hired labour and on indirect taxes, that will complete for you the general picture of our economy'.

'Excuse me, I did not mishear you,' Kremnev inquired, 'you did say your state finances are based on indirect taxes?'

'Quite right,' Alexei Minin smiled, 'you are surprised by such an "old-fashioned" method; it jars in comparison with your American income tax system. But I assure you our indirect taxes are just as progressive as your income brackets. We have enough knowledge of the composition and mechanics of the consumption of all our social strata to arrange the incidence of taxes mainly not on necessities, but on luxury goods, and, besides, the differences between average incomes are not so great. The advantages of indirect taxation is that it does not cost the taxpayer a minute of his time. Our system is altogether so arranged that you may live for years in, say, Volokolamsk *uezd* and not once be reminded of the existence of the State as an oppressive power.

That is not to say that our State organisation is weak. Far from it. It is simply that we stick to methods of operation in which the State refrains from grasping the citizen by the scruff of the neck.

In former times it was very naïvely supposed that the only way to manage the economy was by giving orders, subordinating, nationalising, forbidding, commanding and issuing warrants, in a word, fulfilling the national economic plan by means of pliant performers.

We have always assumed, and can now prove by forty years' experience, that these barbarian trappings, burdensome both to ruler and ruled, are about as necessary now as Zeus's thunderbolts to maintain modern morality. We have long abandoned such methods, just as catapults, battering rams, the semaphore telegraph and the Kremlin walls were abandoned in their own day.

We have much more subtle and effective means of indirect influence, and can always create such conditions for any branch of the economy as to make it meet our requirements.

Later, in a number of practical examples, I shall try to demonstrate to you the strength of our power in the economic sphere.

But now, in concluding my outline of the economy, let me draw your attention to two organisational problems which are particularly important for an understanding of our system.

The first of these is the problem of stimulating economic activity. If you think back to the era of state collectivism and its concomitant reduction of the economy's productive forces, and reflect on the origins of this phenomenon, you will see that its principal causes lay by no means in the state economic plan.

Let us give their due to the organisational skills of Yu. Larin and V. Milyutin: their projects were very well conceived and elaborated in detail.[17] But it is not enough to elaborate, one must also implement; economic policy is the art of implementation par excellence, not the art of planning.

You not only have to design a machine, you also have to find the materials suitable for its construction and the motive power to drive it. You cannot build the Eiffel Tower of straw, nor will two workers put a rotary engine in motion by hand.

When we look at the pre-socialist world, we see that its complex machinery was driven by the power of human greed, by hunger; each component, from the banker to the lowest labourer, drew personal profit from his effort in economic activity, and this interest stimulated his work. Everyone as part of the economic machinery was a motor that kept it in motion.

The Communist system put all participants in economic life on a state wage and so removed all incentive from their work. The fact of work existed, of course, but there was no work effort, for there was nothing to justify it. The lack of incentive affected not only the producers, but also the organisers of production; they, like all officials, were concerned to perfect the economic process, they were concerned with the precise and smooth working of the economic apparatus, but not with the results of its work. To them the appearance of the matter was more important than its practical results.

When we took over the management of the economy, we immediately put in motion all the mechanisms which stimulate private economic activity—piece rates, bonuses for managers and premium prices for those products of peasant farming which it was essential to develop; for example, mulberry farming in the north.

In restoring private economic incentives we had, of course, to be prepared to tackle inequalities in the distribution of the national income.

In this sphere, the main part of the work was already accomplished, since three-quarters of economic activity in regard to industry and trade had been taken over by co-operatives; nevertheless, we were constantly faced with the problem of democratising the national income.

We first turned our attention to reducing the share of unearned income—the principal measures we took were taxing rent in agriculture and the abolition of joint-stock companies and of private finance houses.

I am using the old economic terminology, Mister Charlie, so that you understand what I am talking about, it is still used in your country, but here . . . I wonder whether today's young people know them at all. That was our solution to the economic problem.

The social problem we found much more complex and difficult: how to preserve and develop culture while abolishing towns and high unearned incomes.'

'But now they are calling us to dinner', Alexei's partner stopped his story as he saw through the window that Katerina, with evident pleasure and determination, was striking an iron gong hanging in the midst of the extensive courtyard.

Chapter 10

(In which the fair at White Kolp' is described and the author's complete agreement with Anatole France's dictum that a story without love is like fat without mustard is explained.)

We know, from the surviving 'Book of Expenditure of the Patriarch's Office', that at the beginning of the eighteenth century the Most Holy Patriarch Adrian was daily supplied at table with 'porridge, fresh pike in brine, white sturgeon soup, a dish of stellate sturgeon, cabbage soup and underbelly of fish, fish joints and horseradish, a choice cut of white sturgeon, a pasty with meat' and at least a further twenty dishes in breathtaking quantities and of excellent quality. Comparing this feast of ancient times with the Utopian table in the hospitable house of the Minins, we have to admit that the Patriarch's fare was a little more sumptuous. But only a little . . . Paraskeva had arrived from Moscow and at her bidding such quantities of open pasties and pies, stuffed carp and carp in sour cream and other delicacies appeared on the table that its legs would surely have bent had they been but a little less sturdy; while the socialist politician Kremnev fully expected all the participants in the meal to be dead by the evening from over-indulgence. However, the national dishes prepared for the American's edification vanished rapidly and without trace to the accompaniment of a rising chorus of praise for Paraskeva, who modestly re-addressed it to 'The Russian Cuisine' compiled by Mr Levshin in 1818.[18]

After a nap in the hay-loft in the traditional Orthodox manner, the young people carried Kremnev off to the fair in White Kolp'.

As Kremnev and his companions walked by the banks of the Lama, the shadows of clouds drifted over the mown meadows, flowering rowan bushes made yellow patches along the road, and in the dense autumn air spiders' webs floated about.

Katerina walked along with head held high; a gust of wind outlined clearly the contours of her body against the blue depths of sky beyond the river. Meg and Natasha were picking flowers. There was a smell of autumn wormwood in the air.

'There's the main road!'

They turned onto the highway lined with weeping birches and in the distance they could see the domes of White Kolp' church.

Carts, bright-painted like trays and packed full of lads and lasses cracking nuts, overtook the travellers. The strains of a popular song rang out over the road.

> Little pigeon on the roof-top
> Soon you will be pigeon pie;
> Come and help me, O my darlings,
> Choose the one with whom I'll lie.

Kremnev was surprised by the almost complete absence of any difference between his companions and those who met or overtook them. The same dress and the same Moscow manner of speech and expression. Gaily, and with evident enjoyment, Paraskeva jokingly rebuffed the pleasantries of the passing lads, while Katerina simply hopped into one of the carts, kissed all the girls sitting in it, and took away a bagful of nuts from a surprised youth as she popped a chunk of banana into his mouth.

The fair was in full swing.

Mountains of Tula gingerbreads were piled on a stall, both the crisp variety and that with candied fruit; there were Tver mints in the shape of fishes and of generals and there were the juicy, multicoloured Kolomna fruit-drops.

The passing of centuries had changed nothing in rustic delights, and only a careful observer would have noticed the considerable quantities of preserved pineapple, the bunches of bananas and the extraordinary abundance of good chocolate.

As in the good old days, little boys whistled on gilded clay cockerels, just as they had done in the days of Tsar Ivan Vasilevich and in Novgorod the Great. A double accordion played a fast polka.

In a word, everything was fine.

Katerina, entrusted with the education of Mister Charlie, led him into a large white tent, and without comment pronounced: 'There!'

The walls of the tent were hung with paintings of both old and modern schools. Kremnev joyfully recognised some old friends: Venetsianov, Konchalovskii, Rybnikov's 'St. Hieronimus', the Novgorod 'Elijah' from the Ostroukhov collection, as well as hundreds of new, unfamiliar paintings and sculptures which vividly put him in mind of yesterday's conversation with Paraskeva.[19]

He stopped before 'The Christ child' of Giampietrino which had held him spellbound in the Rumyantsev Museum and, at the risk of destroying his incognito, exclaimed: 'But however did these get to White Kolp' fair?'

Paraskeva hastened to explain that the booth was a touring exhibition from Volokolamsk Museum to which some Moscow paintings had been temporarily loaned.

The densely crowded visitors, looking attentively at the exhibits and exchanging comments, showed Kremnev that the representational arts had become firmly established in everyday peasant life and met with an informed understanding. Of the latter he was further convinced by the rapid rate of sale at the door of the 132nd edition of P. Muratov's *A History of Painting in a Hundred Pages* and the booklet *From Rokotov to Ladonov*,[20] the dust-jacket of which told him that Paraskeva not only could talk about painting, but also wrote books.

In the next tent, peasant women clustered round samples of ancient Russian embroidery, and two lads were sizing up a Boulle cabinet.

Soon the exhibition began to empty; the sound of voices and the ringing of a bell heralded the start of the eurhythmics. This was followed by a knuckle-bone match, a hurdle race and other Yaropole *volost'* championships. Huge blue posters promised 'Hamlet' by Mr Shakespeare at seven o'clock, to be performed by a company from the local co-operative union.

But it was time to hurry home and call in at the bee-garden for some honey on the way. So, abandoning the celebrations, the company only found time to visit the panopticum exhibited by the cultural and educational department of the Guberniya Peasant Union.

Along the walls stood wax busts, portraying historical personages; a panoramic display acquainted the spectators with the major events of national and world history and with the wonders of tropical lands.

Animated exhibits showed Julius Caesar at the Rubicon, Napoleon on the walls of the Kremlin, the abdication and death of Nicholas II, Lenin speaking at the Congress of the Soviets, Sedov routing the typists' rebellion, the basso cantanto Chaliapin and the bass Gaganov.

'Look, but this is your portrait!' Katerina exclaimed.

Kremnev was rooted to the spot. A bust, reminiscent of photographic postcards, stood before him on canvas under a glass. Underneath, the inscription read: 'Alexei Vasil'evich Kremnev, member of the college of the World Economic Council, the suppressor of Russia's peasant movement. According to medical opinion, most probably suffered from persecution mania; degeneration is clearly evidenced by the asymmetry of the face and the structure of the skull.'

Alexei blushed deeply and did not dare look at his companions.

'It's marvellous! An amazing likeness; even the jacket is like yours, Mister Charlie,' cried Nikifor Minin.

Everybody became oddly embarrassed and they left the panopticum tent in silence.

They were in a hurry to get home, but Katerina dragged Kremnev off to the bee-garden for honey. The path cut across some cabbage patches. The intense splashes of their firm, almost blue, heads accentuated the blackness of the earth. Two women, strongly built and wearing white dresses with pink polka-dots, were cutting the ripe ones and throwing them into a two-wheeled cart.

For the first time in his Utopian journey, Alexei, shaken by the confrontation with his waxen double, fully realised the seriousness and hopelessness of his position.

The original sin of his pretended birth bound him hand and foot, while his real name evidently branded him as an outlaw in the land of peasant Utopia.

But this surrounding world of cabbage patches, blue distances and the red rowan clusters was no longer alien to him.

He felt a new and precious bond with it, an affinity even closer than to the socialist world he had left; and the cause of this closeness, Katerina, flushed from the rapid walk, was at his side, spellbound, clinging to him imperceptibly.

They slackened their pace as they descended the steep slope of an old stream. Alexei touched her hand and their fingers intertwined.

The crowns of apple-trees, their boughs bent as in an old Japanese print and laden with fruit, rose in neat rows above the utterly black, freshly tilled earth. Large, red, fragrant apples and the trunks white with lime filled the air with the smell of fertility; the scent seemed to him to soak its way through the pores of his companion's bare hands and neck.

So began his Utopian love.

Chapter 11

(*Very similar to Chapter 9*)

When Kremnev and his companion returned home, supper had long been waiting.

They were greeted coolly, and the company silently sat down to table. There was a feeling of anxiety in the house. The talk was of sinister developments in Germany, of the German Economic Council's demand for a revision of the Galician frontier. It seemed to Alexei that not only he, but also Katerina, felt somehow guilty.

There was also a certain coolness about Alexei Minin when, later in the evening, Alexei went to his study to continue the morning's conversation.

'In our talk today', the grey-haired patriarch began, 'I omitted another peculiarity of our economic system. In striving to democratise the national income it was natural for us to distribute the incoming revenue and it was equally natural to prevent the amassing of large fortunes.

For all its merits, this also had some disadvantages. First, the accumulation of capital was hindered. The distributed revenue was nearly all consumed, and our society's capacity for capital formation was, of course, especially after the abolition of private credit agencies, virtually nil.

So we had to make considerable efforts to get the peasant co-operatives and certain state bodies to take serious steps to create special social capital funds, and thus speed up the process of capital formation. Among these measures is our generous financial support for every kind of inventor and entrepreneur in new areas of economic activity.

Another consequence of the democratisation of national income was a considerable decline in art patronage and the number of people with no occupation, i.e. of the two substrata which to a great extent have nurtured art and philosophy.

But here, too, peasant initiative, with, it must be admitted, some encouragement from the centre, proved equal to the task.

In order to flourish, art needs a high degree of interest on the part of society and an active and generous demand for its works. We now have both; today in White Kolp' you saw the exhibition of paintings and the public's reaction. I should add that, at present, frescoes ordered for the rural building programme are counted in hundreds, if not thousands, of square yards; fine examples of painting can be found in the schools and public buildings of every *volost'*. There is also a considerable private demand.

Do you know, Mister Charlie, that there is a demand not only for the artists' works, but also for the artists themselves? I know of several cases of a *volost'* or *uezd* paying considerable sums on a long-term contract to an artist, a poet or a scientist, just for him to reside in their territory. Not unlike the Medicis and Gonzagas of the Italian Renaissance, you'll agree.

In addition, we give strong support to the Brotherhood of Flor and Lavr, of Olympios the icon-painter, and many others, with the organisation of which you are, I think, already familiar.

As you see, in speaking of the economic problem we have imperceptibly reached the social problem; and this we found more difficult and complicated.

We had to solve the problem of the individual and society. We had to build a human society in which the individual could feel completely unfettered, while society takes care of the common interest by methods invisible to the individual.

And we never allowed society to become an idol or made a fetish of the state.

Our ultimate aim was always the enrichment of human life, an integrated human personality; everything else was a means to that end. We consider society and the state as the most powerful and essential of these means, but never forget that they are no more than means.

We are particularly cautious about the state, which we use only when necessity dictates. The political experience of many centuries unfortunately shows that human nature almost invariably remains human nature; the improvement of manners proceeds with the speed of geological processes. Strong natures, possessed of the will to power, will always seek to make for themselves a full, integrated and meaningful life, but on the ruins of the lives of others. We can fully believe that the life of a Herodes Atticus, a Marcus Aurelius or a Vasilii Golitsyn was scarcely less rich or profound than the lives of our best contemporaries.[21] The only difference is that, then, such lives were lived by a few individuals, while today they are the lot of tens of thousands — and of millions, I hope, in the future. All social progress merely consists in extending the circle of those who drink at the fountain-head of culture and life. Nectar and ambrosia have ceased to be the food of the Olympians alone, they now enrich the homes of humble villagers.

Society has been unswervingly developing in the direction of this progress for the past two centuries and, of course, it has the right to defend itself. When some strong natures, or even whole groups of strong natures, hinder this progress, then society may defend itself, and the state is a well-tried tool for this purpose.

It is also not a bad instrument for a whole number of technical needs.

You'll ask how the state is organised here? As you know, the form of states develop not logically, but historically. This, partly, accounts for many of our existing institutions. The system, as you know, is a Soviet system, a system of peasant councils. On the one hand, it is a heritage of the socialist period of our history; on the other, it has many merits. It should be noted that, among the peasants, it long predates October 1917, when it essentially existed in the management of the cooperatives.

The basic principles of this system are probably known to you, and I shall not dwell on them.

I'll only say that we value in it the idea of the direct responsibility of all authorities to the social groups or organisations which they serve. Only the courts, the organs of state control and some bodies in the communications field are exempt from this rule and are run entirely by central authority.

We see a particular value in the division of legislative power; under this, questions of principle are decided by the Congress of Soviets, having been first considered at local level, and I stress considered, since the law forbids imperative mandates for the delegates. The actual mechanics of legislation are entrusted to the Central Executive Committee and, in some cases, to the Council of People's Commissars.

This method of administration involves the masses very closely in state activity and at the same time ensures flexibility of the legislative machinery.

But in any case we are no sticklers for formality in putting even such a mechanism into effect, and local variants are readily allowed; thus we have parliamentarianism in Yakutsk *oblast'*, while the monarchists of Uglich have set up a local prince, restricted, it is true, in his power, by the local Soviet of Deputies; on the other hand, in the Mongolo-Altai territory, a "governor-general" appointed by the central authority rules alone.'

'Excuse me,' Kremnev interrupted, 'the Congresses of Soviets, the Central Executive Committee and the local Soviets of Deputies—all these merely legitimise power. But on what is real power founded here?'

'Ah, my very dear Mister Charlie, our fellow citizens have almost forgotten about such concerns, for we have stripped the state of virtually all social and economic functions, and the ordinary man has hardly any contact with it.

And, generally, we consider the state to be an outdated mode of organising social life and nine-tenths of our work is done by social methods; it is they that are characteristic of our system: various societies, co-operatives, congresses, leagues, newspapers, other organs of public opinion, academies and, finally, clubs—that is the social fabric which constitutes the life of the nation.

And it is here, in managing it, that we meet exceedingly complicated organisational problems.

Human nature, alas, inclines to go back to the simple life; left to itself, with no social contact or external psychological stimulation, it gradually fades and dissipates its content. A man cast into the forest goes wild. His mind is gradually emptied of content.

Quite understandably, therefore, in fragmenting the towns which had been the spring-heads of culture for many centuries, we were much afraid that, scattered amidst the forests and fields, the rural population would putrify and lose its culture as it did in the Petersburg period of our history.

To combat this putrescence we had to provide for social drainage.

Even greater fears attached to the problem of the future development of culture, of that creative activity which, again, had been due to the towns.

We were constantly dogged by the thought: are the higher forms of culture possible with a population scattered in the countryside?

The era of landlord culture of the 1820s, which produced the Decembrists and gave Pushkin to the world, told us that, technically, all this was possible.

It remained only to find sufficiently powerful technical means.

We made every effort to create a perfect communications network, found ways of making the population use it, at least to go to the local centres, and we flung into these centres all the elements of culture we possessed: the *uezd* and *volost'* theatre, the *uezd* museum and its *volost'* branches, people's universities, every kind of sporting activity, choral societies; everything, even the church and politics, was thrown into the countryside to raise the level of its culture.

We risked much, but for several decades we kept the countryside in a state of psychological tension. A special League for the Organisation of Public Opinion set up dozens of mechanisms for stimulating and maintaining the social dynamism of the masses; I'll even confess that draft laws threatening peasant interests were specially introduced in legislative bodies, in order to arouse peasant social consciousness.

But perhaps the law on obligatory travel for young men and women, and the two-year conscription for military and labour service played the biggest part in bringing our fellow citizens to the fountain-head of culture.

The idea of journeying, borrowed from the medieval guilds, allowed a young man to see the world and expanded his horizons. He was polished still further during his military service. Quite honestly, we attached to it almost no strategic significance; in case of foreign aggression, we have means of defence more powerful than all the guns and cannon taken together; and if the Germans carry out their threats, they will soon discover that.

But the educational value of labour service as a moral discipline is immeasurable. Sports, rhythmic gymnastics, eurythmics, factory work, marches, manœvres, navvying — all this helps to mould our citizens and, verily, militarism of this sort redeems many a sin of the old militarism.

There remains the development of culture; I have already told you something of what has been done in this area.

The main idea which eased the solution of the problem for us was the concept of artificially selecting talented individuals and promoting the organisation of their lives.

In the past there was no scientific understanding of human life; no attempt was made to formulate a science either of its normal development or of its pathology; we knew nothing of the diseases in men's biographies, we had no notion of the diagnosis and treatment of unsuccessful lives.

Those with a feeble stock of potential energy often burnt out like candles and perished, crushed by circumstances; individuals with enormous strength failed to use one tenth of their energy. Today we understand the morphology and dynamics of human life; we know how all the forces inherent in a man can be developed. There are special associations, large and powerful, which have millions of people under their observation; you can rest assured that today not a single talent can be lost, not a single human potentiality will vanish into oblivion . . .'

Shaken, Kremnev leapt up.

'But this is horrible! This is the worst of all tyrannies! These associations of yours that resurrect the German anthroposophists and the French freemasons are the equal of any state terror. Why have a state, indeed, when your whole set-up is no more than a sophisticated oligarchy of a couple of dozen very clever and ambitious men.'

'Calm yourself, Mister Charlie; firstly, any strong personality will feel not the slightest hint of our tyranny; and, second, you would have been right about thirty years ago — then our system was an oligarchy of gifted enthusiasts. Today we are able to say: "Now let Thy servant depart". The peasant masses have learnt to play an active part in shaping the country's public opinion; and if, morally, we are in power, it is only because, as the Germans say, "Und der Kaiser absolut, wenn er unser Wille tut".

Let any organisation, no matter how strong, try to go against the opinion of those who live and reason in the cottages of Yaropolets, Murinovo and thousands of other places, and it'll immediately lose its influence and moral authority.

Believe me, once the people's spiritual culture has reached a certain very high level, it maintains itself automatically and acquires internal stability. Our task is to ensure that each *volost'* should have its own creative cultural life, that the life of Korchevskii *uezd* should not differ qualitatively from that of Moscow *uezd*; having achieved that we, the enthusiasts of rural renaissance, we, the followers of the great prophet, A. Evdokimov, can calmly go to our graves.'

The old man's eyes burnt with the fires of youth; Kremnev was facing a fanatic.

Kremnev rose and turned to Minin with evident irritation.

'All right, you say that the free human individual, the whole state, duty, society, all these are means. Then, in your opinion, is a social criterion for judging their own actions necessary or superfluous for your citizens?'

'For convenience in managing the state, and as a characteristic of the masses, it is desirable, but from an ethical viewpoint it is not essential.'

'And you preach such views openly?'

'I wish you would understand, my dear fellow,' the old man flared up, 'that if we don't have theft, it is not because everyone recognises it is wrong to steal, but because no thought of stealing can arise in our fellow citizens' heads. In our view, if you like, conscious ethics are immoral.'

'All right, but what about you, aware of all this, you, the heads of spiritual life and of society? What are you? Augurs or fanatics to duty? What ideas inspired you to work to create this peasant paradise?'

'Unhappy man!' Alexei Minin exclaimed, drawing himself up to his full height. 'What inspired us, and thousands like us, to work? Ask Scriabin what inspired him to compose "Prometheus", what made Rembrandt create his fabulous visions. It was the sparks of Prometheus' creative flame, Mister Charlie! You want to know what we are, augurs or fanatics of duty? Neither one, nor the other — we are artists.'

Chapter 12

(Describing the considerable improvement in Moscow's museums and places of entertainment and cut short by an exceedingly unpleasant surprise.)

Next morning, Kremnev became conscious of a still greater coolness on the part of the inhabitants of the White Kolp' townlet. There was a reluctance about Alexei Minin as he explained to him the structure of the meteorophore system.

According to his account, a link between the state of the weather and the intensity of magnetic lines of force had been observed as early as the nineteenth century. The passing cyclones and anti-cyclones always had their magnetic counterpart. What was not altogether clear was which was the determining factor: did the weather determine the state of the magnetic field, or the magnetic field determine the weather? Analysis confirmed the second hypothesis; a network of 4,500 magnetic power stations was set up and this allowed almost complete control of the magnetic field, and thus of the weather. Minin went on to describe the meteorophore, but noticing Alexei's weak mathematics, abruptly broke off his explanation . . .

At lunch, Kremnev felt that his position was insupportable and disaster approached; he was therefore immeasurably pleased when Paraskeva asked him to accompany her to Moscow for shopping and to attend a liturgical concert on the Moscow bells.

The light aerocutter set them down at the central aerodrome by 3 o'clock and, as a good hour remained before the concert, Paraskeva proposed that they take a look at the Moscow museums; she said they had now succeeded in doing what the great revolution had been powerless to achieve, and had rescued all their treasures of the spirit from the vaults and the museum routine.

'Even the Historical Museum was finally dragged from under its bushel in 1970!'

The new building of the Rumyantsev Museum occupied a whole huge block, from the Manège to the Znamenka, the front facing the Alexandrov Gardens. Down the long galleries, there opened before them the wonderful visions of Sandro Botticelli, Rubens, Velasquez and other old masters, Japanese enamels and Chinese ones he had not previously known. All these, as Paraskeva explained, were gifts of other lands, exchanged with museums in the West and the East for Novgorod and Suzdal' icons. Rapidly scanning through dozens of rooms, Alexei found himself lingering in the historic relics section. He was struck by Pushkin's room; better than all the dozens of books he had once read about him, it revealed to Alexei the great poet's soul. There was the Ushakov album, the sheets of autograph-book verses, the portraits of his loved ones, the little house at Nashchokino and hundreds more tokens of a life of greatness.

He was overcome by the rooms devoted to the times of the great revolution, where familiar faces and objects, somewhat becobwebbed by time, stared at him with emphatic defiance.

But they could tarry no longer; the first bell was to ring in half an hour.

When they came out into the street, dense crowds filled the squares, parks and gardens along the Moskva. From a programme handed to him, Alexei learnt that the Alexander Smagin Society, to celebrate the harvest festival, invited the Moscow *oblast'* peasants to hear the following programme to be performed on the Kremlin bells in co-operation with those of other Moscow churches.[22]

PROGRAMME

1. Sixteenth-century Rostov peals.
2. Rachmaninov's *Mass*.
3. Ioakim's peals (1731).
4. Borisyak's chimes.
5. A rising Georgii with a falling peal.
6. Scriabin's *Prometheus*.
7. Moscow peals.

A moment later a deep stroke of the Polyelei bell boomed forth and rolled over the city, followed by the answering chords of Kadashi, St. Nicholas of the Great Cross and the Monastery of the Immaculate Conception; the Rostov peal enveloped the whole of Moscow.[23] The metallic sounds floating down over the heads of the silent crowd were like the wing-beat of some mysterious bird. The elemental swirl of the Rostov peal completed its round and gradually rose away into the clouds, as the bells of the Kremlin intoned the austere scales of Rachmaninov's Mass.

Alexei, overwhelmed and prostrated by this solemnisation of high art, felt someone take him by the arm.

Turning quickly, he saw Katerina signalling to him with a secret air to follow her . . . He tried to say something to her, but his voice was drowned without trace by the ringing.

In a moment they were entering the gigantic 'Julia and the Elephant' restaurant in whose rooms one could take refuge from the sound of the bells.

'I don't know who you are,' whispered an agitated Katerina, 'I only know you are not Charlie Mann.'

And, excited and confused, she told him that his bad English pronunciation and pure Russian speech, the details of his dress and his ignorance of mathematics had from the very first day aroused the family's suspicion, which had been steadily growing; that he was now definitely considered to be an anthroposophist aiding the German adventure; that he was in danger of arrest, or worse; that she did not believe this slander; that in the past two days she had come to know and love him; that he was an out-of-the-ordinary man, predatory and beautiful, like a wolf; that she had searched for him to warn him and begged him now to escape; that she was frightened she might put on his track the judicial authorities which were at this moment arresting Germans and anthroposophists; that war would be declared any minute; and, kissing him unexpectedly on the forehead, she disappeared just as unexpectedly.

Kremnev, who had spent years living underground in Russia under the autocracy, was nevertheless bewildered and mortified by his inextricable situation. He shuddered as he noticed the waiters watching him fixedly and with suspicion.

Quickly he went out of the restaurant into the square. The bells no longer shook the sky and the crowds were dispersing in alarm. Boys were scattering news sheets. 'War, war' was heard on every side.

Kremnev had not gone a dozen paces before a heavy hand was clapped on his shoulder and a voice said: 'Stop, comrade, you are under arrest.'

Chapter 13

(Acquainting Kremnev with the bad organisation of places of con-finement in the land of Utopia and with certain forms of Utopian judicial procedure.)

The spacious 'Hotel for Visitors from Ryazan'', temporarily converted into a prison was surrounded on all sides by patrols of the Peasant Guard in the picturesque costume of the musketmen of Alexei Mikhailovich's time.

When the commissar who had arrested Alexei brought him into the lobby and handed him over to the commandant, the latter took his arrest number, rang the hall-porter, and then said:

'We've made a bit of a miscalculation about rooms and I shall have to put you in a common dormitory for tonight. You seem to have no luggage. If you are from Moscow, let me have the address, and we'll send home for what you need.'

Kremnev said that, unfortunately, he was a visitor, and they promised to get him everything from the hotel's stock.

The hotel's concert hall, adapted as a prison cell, resembled a railway terminus in the good old days. Men and women of every condition and age sat by their travelling bags and bundles in attitudes of boredom and with gloomy faces.

There were Germans in leather jackets and caps, thin and slender, with their Teutonic superiority and disdain for their surroundings. There were pale Russian ladies, young men with unseeing, colourless eyes, and agile individuals of uncertain oriental origin.

As Alexei later discovered, the Russian ladies and the young men were anthroposophists, unfortunates caught up in the German intrigue, who had succumbed to the great German idea.

The prison commandant came into the hall and again apologised to the assembly for their deprivation of liberty and the intolerable accommodation; he expressed the hope that all would be free in a couple of days, and promised to make up for the inconvenience by a good meal and various entertainments.

In fact, the dinner, or rather supper, was not long delayed, and afterwards the Germans crowded round the card-tables to gamble the evening away, while the rest of the public heard a miniature concert hastily organised by the commandant.

They slept on camp beds, without undressing. In the morning Alexei was interrogated. When asked who he was and why he pretended to be the American engineer Charlie Mann, he frankly told his whole story, and fearful that his tale would be met with ridicule, offered as proof his bust in the White Kolp' panopticum and the reliable evidence contained in the historic relic galleries of the Rumyantsev Museum.

To his great astonishment, his tale encountered neither opposition nor incomprehension, but was calmly noted down and he was told that in the evening he would be handed over for expert investigation.

The whole, exhaustingly long day Kremnev sat before the windows of the room he had been allocated and looked at the town.

The social sea was in turmoil; like Old Man Black Sea, rural Russia was bringing forth from its depths thirty-three heroic forces.

Along the roadway before his windows, columns of troops in close formation marched with the rapid step of the French chasseurs. Some young lady, in blue riding-dress and a general's plume, was mounted on a white horse to take the parade of the women's light cavalry. Alexei's heart raced when he recognised Katerina's well-known features at the head of one of the squadrons passing by. Soon infantry replaced the cavalry and throngs of civilians filled every space in sight.

The crowd listened to orators who addressed it from moving cars and clutched at the sheaves of telegram tape that were scattered into the streets.

Towards evening, Alexei was put in a closed car and taken to the Mokhovaya, where the committee of experts awaited him in the circular hall of the university senate.

'Tell us,' a grey-haired old man in gold-rimmed glasses began his questioning, 'what is *Oblikomzap*? If you are really a contemporary of the great revolution, you should be able to explain the meaning of this word.'

Kremnev replied with a smile that it meant the Oblast' Executive Committee of the Western Oblast', a body which existed for a time in St. Petersburg after the capital had been transferred to Moscow.

What kind of institution was the *tsekmonkul't*?

The Central Committee of Monopolised culture, established in 1921 for the compulsory utilisation of cultural forces.

'Tell us what were the reasons for the forcible establishment and the subsequent abolition of the Committees of Poor Peasants?'

Kremnev replied quite adequately to this question, too.

He was shown a series of documents of the period and asked to comment on them; this he also did satisfactorily and, finally, he was obliged to explain, with difficulty and at length, the idea of the urbanisation of agriculture, in reply to a question on state farms.

The outcome was that professorial interrogators shook their heads long and regretfully and informed him that, though undoubtedly he was well-read in the revolutionary literature, and had evidently familiarised himself with the archives, he was entirely unrepresentative of the spirit of the period and, from ignorance, monstrously misinterpreted historical events; he could thus in no case be acknowledged to be their contemporary.

When Alexei was driven back to the prison, the streets again seethed with a crowd that roared loudly and triumphantly, like the sea.

Chapter 14

(And the last of the first part, which demonstrates both that sometimes ploughshares may successfully be turned into swords and that Kremnev finally turned out to be in an exceedingly piteous situation.)

The triumphant and resonant ringing of bells woke the unwilling residents of the 'Hotel for Visitors from Ryazan'' and they were soon informed that, the war being over, they were all free, but those who wished could stay for morning coffee.

The prison at once became a busy hotel, thus recovering its primary nature.

When Kremnev was leaving, the commandant handed him a packet with the findings of the investigating committee; these stated that, in the absence of evidence of a crime, the citizen calling himself Alexei Kremnev should be freed along with the rest. The committee considered his account of his origins improbable, but, finding no grounds to impute a criminal intent to the self-styled citizen Kremnev's imposture, was closing the investigation instigated by Nikifor Minin.

Alexei decided to exercise his right to breakfast at state expense on the terrace of his former prison and, sitting down at a table, he buried himself in the official account of the ending of war in a news sheet flung to him by a paper seller.

Alexei learnt that, on 7th September, three armies of German conscripts, accompanied by swarms of aeroplanes, had invaded the Russian Peasant Republic, and within twenty-four hours, without meeting any signs of resistance, or indeed of life, had penetrated to distances of 30, and in places 70, miles into its territory.

At 3.15 a.m. on 8th September, in accordance with a predetermined plan, the frontier-zone meteorophores exerted the maximum intensity of lines of force on a cyclone of small diameter; in the course of half an hour the millions-strong armies, and tens of thousands of aeroplanes, were literally swept away by monstrous whirlwinds. A wind curtain was established on the frontier and the Tara aerosleds gave such assistance as was possible to the defeated hordes. In two hours, the Berlin government announced that it was ceasing hostilities and would pay any compensation required for damage it had caused.

The form chosen by the Russian Council of People's Commissars was some dozens of canvases by Botticelli, Domenico Veneziano and Holbein together with the Pergamon altar, and 1,000 Chinese coloured engravings of the T'ang period, as well as 1,000 pedigree stud bulls of the famous 'Nur für Deutschland' breed.

The resounding trumpets of the peasant army played fanfares and the sounds of Scriabin's *Prometheus*, which turned out to be the national anthem, shook the Moscow sky.

His coffee drunk, his roast-beef finished, Kremnev rose from his chair. Hunched and dejected by his experience, he slowly came down the steps of the terrace, walking alone, friendless and penniless, to face life in a Utopian country he hardly knew.

NOTES

1. N. A. Demchinskii (1851–1915) and his son B. N. Demchinskii (1877–?).
2. V. V. Flerovskii, pseudonym of V. V. Bervi (1829–1918).
3. *i.e.* an acronym, modelled on many actual Soviet examples, for the Chief Paper Board.

4. The Sukharevka was a market where virtually anything could be acquired, at a price.
5. Chayanov here evidently refers to William Morris, Sir Thomas More, the American Edward Bellamy (1850–98) and Robert Blatchford (1851–1943), editor of *The Clarion*.
6. The quotation is from Herzen's *From the Other Shore*, chap. VII.
7. P. N. Milyukov (1859–1943), a historian, was a member of the Kadet Party.
   P. I. Novgorodtsev (1866–1924) was a lawyer and historian.
   E. D. Kuskova (1869–1958) was a member of the Kadet and later of the Socialist Revolutionary parties, a publicist and wife of S. N. Prokopovich (see note 11). She was expelled from Russia in 1922.
   N. P. Makarov (1886–?), an agrarian economist, was a member of the League of Agrarian Reform.
8. V. V. Sher (1884–?) was a Communist administrator.
   D. B. Ryazanov (pseudonym of Goldenbakh) (1870–1938) was a Social-Democrat, later a Bolshevik, and was for a time Director of the Marx-Engels Institute.
   E. D. Kushova (1869–1958) was a member of the Kadet and later of the Socialist Revolutionary parties, a publicist and wife of S. N. Prokopovch (see note 8). She was expelled from Soviet Russia in 1922.
9. I. P. Vitali was the sculptor who, in 1835, produced the bronze figures for a fountain in Theatre Square. The First Printer was Ivan Fedorov, who printed books in Russia for the first time in 1564; there is a statue to him by the Kitai-gorod wall.
10. These were the leaders of the Bolsheviks, the Provisional Government and the Kadet Party.
11. A. I. Rykov (1881–1938) was a Bolshevik, twice a member of the Supreme Council of the National Economy, who became Prime Minister after Lenin. A. I. Konovalov was Kerenskii's deputy in the Provisional Government, and later a White emigré. S. N. Prokopovich (1871–1955) was an economist, a Social Democratic member of the Provisional Government, later banished from the USSR. S. P. Sereda (1871–1933) was Bolshevik Commissar of Arable Farming from April 1918 to December 1921 and S. L. Maslov (1867–1946), a Socialist-Revolutionary, had been the last Minister of Agriculture in the Provisional Government.
12. Probably Pierre Picart, a Dutch engraver who worked in Russia in the seventeenth and early eighteenth century.
13. I. V. Zheltovskii (1867–1959) was an architect involved in a plan for the intended reconstruction of Moscow after 1918.
14. The Moscow City People's University was founded by a bequest from General A. L. Shanyavskii (1837–1905) in 1908. In 1912, Chayanov had published a brief account of it under the title *Istoriya Miusskoi ploshchadi*. It was abolished in 1918.
15. K. B. Radek (pseudonym of Sobelson) (1885–1939) was a member of various European Social-Democratic parties before joining the Russian Communist Party.
16. Gustave Hervé (1871–1944) was a French socialist.
17. Yu. Larin (pseudonym of M. A. Lur'e) (1882–1932) was an economist. V. P. Milyutin was the first Bolshevik Commissar of Arable Farming in November–December 1917, then a member of the Supreme Council of the National Economy.
18. V. A. Levshin (1746–1826), a prolific translator and author, had issued a six-part 'Cook's Calendar' in 1808.
19. A. G. Venetsianov (1780–1847) is regarded as the first Russian naturalist painter and the originator of an important genre school.
   P. P. Konchalovskii (1876–1942) was a realist painter.
   I. S. Ostroukhov was a late nineteenth-century art collector and patron. His collection was nationalised after 1917.
20. F. S. Rokotov (1735 or 1736–1809) was a portrait painter.

21. Vasili Golitsyn (1643–1714) was an outstanding Russian statesman who dealt mainly with foreign affairs.

22. Aleksandr Vasil'evich Smagin (1843–?), was a peasant from the Perm region who became a famous bellringer and expert on Russian campanology.

23. The main Rostov bells were cast when Iona was metropolitan there, from 1652 to 1691. Polyelei, the 'much-anointed', was the name of one of these bells, weighing over sixteen tons, and cast in 1682 by Filipp Andreev. Chayanov's sixteenth-century peal is thus either an anachronism, or a mistake for 'seventeenth-century.' The Iona or Sysoi peal was the first of the three full Rostov peals; this peal is perhaps referred to in item 1 of the programme. The others were those of Ioakim and Georgii (see items 3 and 5 in the programme). Ioakim was archbishop at Rostov 1731–41; he had been preceded by Georgii Dashkov as archbishop, 1718–31. Chayanov appears to imply that the Rostov bells had been brought to the Moscow Kremlin by 1984.

The Sign of the Zodiac

The Sign of

Second Evening Edition

Moscow   Friday 5th September 1984

> Yesterday at two o'clock **Arsenii Nikolaevich Bragin** died peacefully.
> Funeral tomorrow noon at the Pantheon of Russian Science.

Military Training Board invites young men and girls born in 1964 to report to their sections on 1st October.

The Fruiterers' Union announces the arrival of: 'Glass Field' grapes
Trebizond bananas

The Sol'vychegodsk Cultural Society is looking for artists and musicians wishing to live in its area. Details from the Secretariat, Sol'vychegodsk Cultural Society.

Stradivarius for sale. Flat 31, 7 Lubyanka.

New 'Anthropophage' books.
1. 'Collected Memoirs of the Great Revolution', with portraits of the authors. 10 grammes of gold.
2. 'The Art of Tying Neckties', with colour illustrations. 5 grammes of gold.
3. Karamzin, 'Letters of a Russian Traveller', illustrated by Ladonov, 4 volumes. 15 grammes of gold.
4. P. Minina, 'From Rokotov to Ladonov', illustrated. 3 grammes of gold.

LATEST NEWS

Dresden.   4 September

Debates in the German Central Executive Committee on the grain situation are becoming increasingly acrimonious. According to a report of the People's Commissariat of Agriculture, despite the fact that the German state farms now sow 55 per cent of their area with legumes, the population of Central Europe must either stop growing or find a new agricultural base to supplement its food supplies. Rumour has it that the continuous closed sessions of the German Central Executive Committee ended with the election of a special supreme committee which has been given exceptional powers to negotiate with the Anglo-French and Russian isolated systems on an international solution to the German food crisis. The proposal by Hageman and the young agrarianists to transfer to a system of peasant farming was rejected by the German Central Executive Committee without debate. The political situation remains extremely tense.

Constantinople. 5 September. LVII Olympic Games. Morning. Jumping, Sidorov 34. Discus, Lautiey 28. Lawn Tennis Semi-Finals, Itala. Cambridge. Street fisticuffs: Paris; boxing: Sydney. Sasaferota, Borsov Oioma.

5th September 1984 23.00 hours

We were right ... regrettably, we were right. Yesterday's speech by Arkhip Taratin has reaped, and could not fail to reap, a bitter harvest. Had our forefathers found their way today into the colonnaded hall of the Central Executive Committee they would have recognised the view of the stormy sea of social passions so characteristic of the past era of urban culture.

Taratin and Co. can rest satisfied. A Spartan system of education carried out by Spartan political methods has produced customs and manners reminiscent of the Persian wars.

the Zodiac

Organ of the O.M.S.K.O.[1]

23.00 hours   Number 234 (b)

Editorial offices Dmitrovka, 26. Telephones 17–37 and 5–29–93 Radio call-sign: LL175 Manuscripts not accepted for publication are not returnable Open 4 to 6 p.m.	Head Office: Krylatskoe Village, Moscow *uezd*. Telephones: 3–04–23 and 47-6. Radio call-sign: E 176 Subscription: 10 grammes of gold. Monthly: 1 gramme of gold. Retail price per issue: 0·4 grammes of gold Advertisements: 0·2 grammes of gold per line

IN THIS ISSUE:

Extraordinary Uproar At Central Executive Committee Session
Germany Faces Famine
Death of Arsenii Bragin
Russian Triumphs at LVII Olympic Games
Chinese Make Petroleum From Air

Fortunately the 'helots' rebelled. The whole programme of the great Arkhip and his supporters is extremely simple.

I, Arkhip, am exceedingly fond of 'stadiums' and 'hippodromes'. For some reason the despicable helots inhabiting Esipleva and the neighbouring *volosts* prefer Gregory the Theologian and the paterikon of the Monastery of the Caves. But we Arkhips are in a majority in the Kineshma Soviet.[2] And since 'there is no power but of God', hear, you heathen, and submit.[3] Let there be a stadium in every *volost*'!!

Is the Kineshma Pericles short of gold to propagate his Attic ideas among the helots? Then let the stupid helots pay 5 grammes per *desyatina* as a special local impost, and let them disport themselves at the Taratin stadiums.

In a word, back to the days of Frederick the Great and Catherine! Back to the late lamented state collectivism! Back to the principles of enlightened absolutism! The framework of the Peasant Soviet Republic is too narrow for expansive natures.

But, most astonishing of all, when Kineshma paternalism causes a national scandal, and when the supreme authority of the higher majority explains to Comrade Taratin that it is its task to protect not only the freedom of the creative leadership, even though it should enjoy the support of a local majority, but the freedom of each citizen, be this 'helot' in the most insignificant minority in his own locality—the Arkhips of this world are genuinely surprised.

The debates reveal that—to the Kineshma Pericles—the foundation of our peasant culture—the great 1928 Decree on the citizen's inalienable individual rights—is but a curious piece of paper displayed as Exhibit No. 37a in the Central Executive Committee's Museum. What is so bad is that two days of legislative work should be wasted, as was the case yesterday and today, on such elementary lessons in political literacy. It would have been far better if our Arkhips, before embarking on state service, had read attentively 'The Fundamentals of Peasant Culture'.

Freedom for authority or freedom from authority

The Kineshma tragi-comedy of Arkhip Taratin and the *volost'* stadiums revives in the columns of our press the endlessly old but eternally new question of ideological authority over the people.

The history of the Jesuits in the seventeenth century, of the freemasons in the eighteenth and nineteenth and of the anthroposophists in the twentieth shows that there exist methods of social manipulation by which a small group of individuals can reduce the broad masses of the people to spiritual slavery. Such organisations, what is more, often do not share the ideas and desires they foist upon the masses, but simply use them as means to the achievement of particular ideological objectives.

When such a danger exists, the question necessarily arises: should not the state authority be the guardian of the people's intellectual life and use all its force to destroy the ideological snares set by these cunning fishers of men and to protect the people against encroachments on their intellectual freedom?

We know that in past centuries this question was answered in the affirmative. The expulsion of the Jesuits, prosecutions against the Masons, religious and political censorship, legislation against socialists—and many other forms of the persecution of ideas were practised intensively and not necessarily ineffectively.

But all these methods of control can hardly be applicable in our peasant system.

Fundamental to our life and culture is its characteristic method of solving social and economic problems by community action, and not by the force of state compulsion. The great decree of 1928 on the citizen's inalienable individual rights made the state into an obedient instrument of human individuality and destroyed the fetish of its sovereign rights. Therefore, the sledge-hammer of state authority comes down only when the exercise of personal freedom violates somebody's inalienable individual rights, when, for example, a father's authority violates his son's right to essential education.

This is the basis of our law on minimum education, a law by which all our schools, by whoever managed, are bound.

But, if the exercise of one's freedom does not violate any other person's inalienable rights, no power can limit this freedom. This is why the whole development of our life and habits must necessarily be cast in a communal mould. This is why we cannot use state authority to control ideological propaganda, as long as it does not violate anyone's freedom and does not directly threaten the existing social structure.

Arkhip Taratin may then exclaim: 'But how can I stop the corrupting influence of Old Believer preaching of a return to seventeenth century monastic retreats?'

'Very simply,' we should answer. 'By methods of community control. Against each evangelist set a preacher of Great Hellas's ideals, but not a policeman in an Achaean helmet.'

The late lamented era of state collectivism was proof positive that there was no Atlas now able alone to support the globe on his shoulders and that an intellectual monopoly can lead to nothing but the extinction of the life of the spirit.

Let us remember that in the life of the spirit only the intellectually weak need to have their ideas protected by extraneous means. If, in the forests of Kostroma, the principles of the Great Attic culture, to which we are so attached, cannot stand up to the Bible-quoting of Fedoseev's followers, that culture is not worth a penny, Arkhip Nikolaevich!

Or, rather, not the Attic culture itself, but its Kostroma manifestation.

You will say that we are advocating 'laissez faire, laissez passer'. No, this principle belonged to capitalist times, that is, an era which is almost prehistory for us.

It is only that in our resolute advance towards the reconstruction of the world according to our ideals, we believe, and have ample experience to bear us out, that our problems do not require the intervention of the thunderbolts of state power, but can be more easily and more firmly resolved by means of voluntary social construction.

The structure of peasant Russia should allow, not so much a freedom for authority to manifest itself, as a freedom from authority.

Aleksei Minin

In memoriam.

Arsenii Bragin, a great sociologist.

A remarkable life has been extinguished. The patriarch of the science which he founded has passed away.

Thirty years ago, when Russian readers opened a thick volume inscribed with the title 'The Rate of Social Change and Methods of Measuring it', Arsenii Bragin was already well-known as a fiery orator of the peasant group in the Central Executive Committee and an exceptionally successful and skilful leader in a wide variety of political campaigns.

His enormous personal experience in the management of social processes and his magnificently effective campaign to organise the political power of the scattered peasantry promised Bragin an exceptional political career. The scholar's study, however, was closer to his heart.

Bragin, who went on from social technology to social theory, was fond of saying that the way to create a science of sociology was, *first*, to accumulate experience in the scientific study of individual practical social problems and, second, to find methods to express social phenomena quantitively.

'The Rate of Social Change' resolved the second problem. 'The Theory of the Creation, Maintenance and Destruction of Reputations', which shortly followed, and the multi-volume 'Theory of Political and Social Forces' pointed the way to a solution of the first.

Having accomplished the entire life's programme which he had sketched out for himself in a youthful note, Arsenii Bragin withdrew from 'activity' and spent the last 12 years in contemplation of the world. Yesterday his life was extinguished like the flame of a burnt-out candle, and tomorrow his friends and pupils will accompany his remains to the Pantheon of Russian Science.

A. Velikanov

Press round up

Among the general chorus of indignant voices against Taratin's outburst at yesterday's Central Executive Committee session, *The People's Will* writes: 'For all the absurdity of Taratin's claim that the CEC has no authority over Kineshma affairs, his speech did raise the major and still unresolved problem of federalism'.

For some people 'twice two' remains an unsolved problem . . .

For the Ivano-Voznesensk *Pravda*, on the other hand, there is no uncertainty at all:

'Taratin's words rang out as the voice of a true statesman in these times of petty parochialism.' Not so beautiful, as true!

The Plough is disturbed by events in Germany, 'threatening complications' 'for a mankind which for forty years has been able to rest from international life'.

The Anthropophage Publishing House has issued a three-volume collection of 'Memoirs of the Great Revolution'. A great part of the material is already familiar to the reading public, but there are some new things; thus we learn that the famous Moscow State Assembly took place at the Bolshoi Theatre against the set of the gamblers' den in 'The Queen of Spades' where 'You today and me tomorrow' is sung.

A few diaries are quoted. We read in one of them of the incredulous surprise of the father of a family in 1919 when his daughter, who was in category I, received 1 pound of sugar for 6 rubles 50 kopecks, while his wife, in category III, received a quarter of a pound for 13 rubles 25 kopecks and so on. We strongly recommend you to read it. Though the events are recent, they seem hard to believe.

A.

Meteorophores: Square 38

Until noon	Clear skies
12—2 p.m.	High temperatures for corn drying
2 p.m.—3 p.m.	Clear skies
3 p.m.—9 p.m.	Clouding over
9 p.m.—3 a.m.	General rain

Central State Bodies

Today in the Central Executive Committee the daily sitting opened at 14.00 hours. Sisipatr Lbov in the chair.[4]

Replying to a question of the Kostroma deputies, the Chairman of the Council of People's Commissars explained that it was true that a system of municipal education similar to that of the Greek gymnasia had been adopted by the Kineshma Soviet, and a special local land tax introduced to finance it; that the Trans-Volga *volosts* had indeed refused to pay this tax and, when the gymnasia and the stadiums attached to them were built, they could not be opened, owing to a total lack of pupils, who chose to remain in the ordinary local schools. The Kineshma Soviet decreed that the construction of the gymnasia should continue and the necessary money be withdrawn from the allocations for road works in those *volosts*. The Trans-Volga *volosts* petitioned that they should be made a separate *uezd*, and at yesterday's session of the Council of People's Commissars this was accepted in principle. (Applause; agitation and shouts of 'Shame!' on the benches of the Kineshma deputies.)

A. Taratin protested against the decision of the Council of People's Commissars. He declared that it violated the federative principle and that the Kineshma commune would not obey it. (Uproar, shouts of 'Shame, shame!' The Chairman calls for order.)

No human society could exist without internal discipline and the sovereign rights of the majority. Therefore, the Kineshma commune, considering that the events in question were an internal affair, could not accept outside interference. (Uproar. Chairman calls for order.)

O. Bulgakov pointed out that, in the name of social discipline, the Kineshma majority should submit to the majority of the whole Republic.

I. Sirotkin declared that the people of Kineshma were not part of the Russian Republic, but members of the federation of Russian independent republics and would defend their political independence with armed resistance if need be. (Uproar. Shouts. Deputies leap from their places. Taratin attempts to explain his colleague's erroneous statement, declaring his words represented Sirotkin's personal opinion. Growing uproar. The Chairman adjourns the sitting until 9.00 p.m.)

At home and abroad

Vologda. 5 September.

After two months' negotiations, with the assistance of the People's Commissariat of Agriculture, an agreement has been reached between the General Union of Peasant Dairymen and the General Bureau of Regional Consumer Unions on price levels for dairy products in 1985. Obstacles to the conclusion of a general contract have been overcome and the crisis over dairy supplies can be considered at an end.

Urga. 5 September.

Professor Ty-phoo Tea[5] of the University of Panch-Ki has discovered a cheap industrial method for the irradiation of nitrogen giving a 60 per cent yield of benzol hydro-carbons. After hearing Ty-phoo Tea's report, the United Soviet of the Asiatic Provinces decided to award him the title of Mi-Ta-Ta-Fui which means 'Conqueror of the Fuel Famine'.

Arts and Sciences

The Olympios the Icon-Painter Society is arranging a Pieter Brueghel commemoration exhibition of paintings by its members. It is stipulated that the paintings should be in Pieter Brueghel's range of colour and forms. The preview will be next Sunday in the exhibition halls of the Rumyantsev Museum.

The Union of Peasant Choral Societies intends to perform Mozharov's 'The land brings forth live shoots' on 1st May next year with a united chorus drawn from the 32 Great Russian provinces with 40,000 singers. Scores are being distributed to the *volost'* departments of the Union.

Vilbrand's historical researches have finally established that the author of the well-known political pamphlet of the 1920s, 'Gruel for the peasant, or the peasant for gruel', was N. Oganovskii.[6]

Here and there

The report of the Ryazan' Social Fund has been published; the fund now stands at 120 tons of gold.

It is rumoured that certain members of the Committee on Indirect Taxation and Prices have proposed to subsidise the cultivation of legumes from taxes on sunflower oil, against the inflated price of which there are complaints from the north.

From 1st October the evening trans-Atlantic air flight from the Western Aerodrome will depart at 20.00 hours.

A patient with a rare complaint has been brought to a Moscow clinic from Smolensk Guberniya. He is suffering from a condition reminiscent of 'typhus', a disease widespread at the time of the great revolution. No cases have been reported in the last 50 years.

Books! New! Books!

Anon., *Story of Car No. 2734*. A historical novel, Moscow, 1984, VII + 1230 pp., 5 grammes of gold.

This is the most attractive book of this year's literary harvest.

Admittedly, its historical truth is no more than a probability, but it is similar to many brilliant aphorisms and does not pretend to be anything more. The author tells how a Sistley car crossed the ocean under threat of German submarines and ended up in the Imperial palace garages in the snow-bound Petrograd of 1916. It made its debut rocking the miserable Alice[7] on its springs; a few months later it whirled away the bloody corpse of Rasputin onto the Little Nevka; it was seized by the Volynians at the corner of Liteinii Prospect on 26th February 1917; it faithfully and truly served Chkheidze, Tereshchenko, Chernov and Tsereteli[8]; it was requisitioned from the latter by sailors. On 3rd July 1917 it took part in the bloody epic of the July Days; afterwards, in October, it went to Moscow with two young men, whose names history has not preserved, and for many years rocked on its springs the venerable Bonch-Bruevich. The ephemeral owners of the car, chance passengers and drivers pass before the reader in colourful procession. Accurate descriptions and finely outlined portraits of historic personalities and nameless servitors at the court, SR agitators, singers, communist commissars and politics-mongering professors, fill the pages of the novel which ends its round with an intensely realistic picture of the old woman Pelageya taking the co-op's milk cans to the railway station from the village of Belozerovo on the old and battered chassis.

Bookworm

A. Velikanov. '*The Development of Peasant Public Opinion in the Twentieth Century*', 5th edition, supplemented and revised, Moscow 1984, XII + 400 pp. 8 grammes of gold.

With admirable persistence, the author continues to exploit a new historical source in the study of the human spirit. His basic idea—that to understand a period it is essential to study the ideas and views, not of its famous thinkers, but of the common citizen—has led him to bundles of ordinary letters, to the simple jottings of diaries. The Bragin school established the general method of dealing with such material, and now we see before us the depths of national life, the subsoil of history. The 5th edition is expanded by 50 new pages and enriched by 10 portraits, among them the particularly interesting description of the peasant Kuzmichev, whose recently found diary throws light on the period of the first Peasant Council of People's Commissars.

T.

Theatres

Opening tomorrow

Bolshoi Theatre Moscow 'Hassan of Bari', an opera by Anatolii Aleksandrov.

Arts Theatre—In memory of Stanislavskii —'Kamargo and the seven Dutchmen', a comedy by Scorpiolanti.

Western Hall 'Hamlet' by Shakespeare. Other programmes as advertised.

Lost on the Lubyanka yesterday, a bundle of manuscripts. Please return to Klepikov, 7 Tverskoi Boulevard.[9]

Published by O.M.S.K.O.

Editor: P. I. Galkin

EDITOR'S NOTES

1. An acronym probably meaning 'Amalgamated Moscow Union of Peasant (or, possibly, Co-operative) Societies', assuming the initials stand for *Ob"edinennyi Moskovskii Soyuz krest'yanskikh/kooperativnykh obshchestv.*

2. Kineshma *uezd* was the fourth most populated *uezd* in Kostroma *guberniya,* according to the 1897 census. The *guberniya* then had a population of 1,429 thousands; Kineshma *uezd* had 148 thousands.

3. Romans, XIII, 1.

4. Sisipatr Lbov, i.e. Saving Father Lbov, might be taken to refer to Prince V. N. Lvov, head of the Provisional Government in Russia until July, 1917. The surname, however, derived from the word for forehead, also suggests something like 'Dunder-head' or 'Dolt'. Perhaps, though, it should be understood both in this sense and as a reference to Lenin—the Saving Father with the prominent forehead.

5. Cadbury Typhoo Ltd. state that 'nowhere in our Archives can we find reference either to this gentleman or the . . . . phantasy that you mentioned and we certainly have no association with Moscow in 1984'.

6. N. Oganovskii was the author of several works on Russian agrarian matters in the first quarter of this century. In 1917 he and Chayanov had edited a statistical handbook on the agrarian question.

7. *I.e.* Alix of Hesse-Darmstadt, known in Russia as Aleksandra Fedorovna, wife of Nicholas II.

8. N. S. Chkheidze (1864-1926) was a Menshevik leader who emigrated from Russia in 1921.

   M. I. Tereshchenko (1886-?) was a liberal; he had been Minister of Finance and Minister of Foreign Affairs in the Provisional Government. He emigrated after October 1917.

   V. M. Chernov (1876-1952) a leader of the Socialist Revolutionaries who emigrated from Russia in 1920.

   I. G. Tsereteli (1882-1959) a leading Menshevik who emigrated from Russia in 1921.

9. S. A. Klepikov edited a volume on Russian agricultural statistics in 1923.

Russian Terms

Administrative areas (in descending order of importance):

guberniya
uezd
volost'

		British equivalents	Metric
Length			
	versta	0·66 miles	1·07 km.
	arshin	28·00 inches	71 cm.
Area			
	desyatina	2·7 acres	1·09 hectares
Weight			
	pud	36 lb.	16·38 kg.
	pound (Russian)	0·9 lb.	0·41 kg.
Liquid measure			
	vedro	21·6 Imperial pints	12·3 litres

Bibliography

Alliluyeva, Svetlana, 1969, *Only One Year*, London.
Bednyi, D., 1922, 'Gnetuchka', *Pravda*, No. 160, 20 July.
Bogolepov, M., 'Gosudarstvennoe khozyaistvo (1892–1903g.)', in *Istoriya Rossii v XIXv.*, VIII: 1–66.
Bol'shakov, A. M. 1924a, *Sovetskaya derevnya (1917–1924gg.), ekonomika i byt*, Leningrad.
Bol'shakov, A. M., 1924b, *Vspomogatel'nye istoricheskie distsipliny*, 4-e izd., Leningrad.
Bol'shakov, A. M., 1927, *Derevnya, 1917–27*, Moscow.
Bol'shakov, A. M., N. A. Rozhkov, 1925, *Khrestomatiya po istorii khozyaistva Rossii*, Leningrad.
Bondarenko, V., 1964, 'Veka i desyatiletiya', *Grani*, No. 56:188–204.
Botanik X. [A. V. Chayanov], 1918, *Istoriya parikmakherskoi kukly ili Poslednyaya lyubov' Moskovskago arkhitektora M.*, Moscow.
Botanik X [A. V. Chayanov], 1923, *Venetsianskoe zerkalo ili Dikovinnye pokhozhdeniya steklyannogo cheloveka*, Berlin.
Brown, E. J., 1976, *Brave New World, 1984, and We*, Ann Arbor.
Chayanov, A. V., 1967, *A. V. Chayanov on the Theory of Peasant Economy* (ed. D. Thorner, B. Kerblay, R. E. F. Smith), Homewood, Ill.
Chertkov, L. N., 1975, 'Chayanov, A. V.', *Kratkaya literaturnaya entsiklopediya*, VIII. 448–9, Moscow.
Davies, R. W., 1958, *The Development of the Soviet Budgetary System*, Cambridge.
Deutscher, I., 1955, ' '1984'—the mysticism of cruelty', *Heretics and Renegades*, London.
ERDE [i.e. RD], 1922, 'Ot velikogo do smeshnogo . . . . ili ne v svoi sani ne sadis'', *Izvestiya*, No. 93, 28 April:3.
Fortunatov, A. F., 1893, *Sel'skokhozyaistvennaya statistika evropeiskoi Rossii*, Moscow.
Gorki, M., 1922a, 'Le paysan russe' (trad. par Andre Pierre), *Revue politique et litteraire, Revue bleue*, Paris:533–6, 576–9 and 613–8.
Gorki, M., 1922b, 'Anarchia', *Il Secolo*, Milan, 2 April.
    1922c, 'Crudeltà', *Il Secolo*, Milan, 4 April.
    1922d, 'Scetticismo', *Il Secolo*, Milan, 6 April.
    1922e, 'Il domani', *Il Secolo*, Milan, 9 April.
Gorki, M., 1925, *Lenine et le paysan russe* (trad. par Michel Dumesnil de Gramont), Paris.
Gor'kii, M., 1922a, 'Chto budet s Rossiei? (O russkom narode)', *Rupor*, Sofia, No. 1:4–6.
    1922b, *Novaya Rossiya*, No. 2: 141–4.
    1922c, 'Gorki om Rusland', *Politiken*, Copenhagen, 2 April.
    1922d, 'Den russiske Grusomhed', *Politiken*, Copenhagen, 4 April.
    1922e, 'Den russiske Bondes Tro', *Politiken*, Copenhagen, 6 April.
    1922f, 'Den russiske Bonde og Fremtiden', *Politiken*, Copenhagen, 9 April.
    1922g, *O russkom krest'yanstve*, Berlin.
Gorky, M., 1968, *Untimely Thoughts, Essays on Revolution, Culture and the Bolsheviks 1917–1918*, trans. H. Ermolaev, New York.
Gross, Miriam, ed., 1971, *The World of George Orwell*, London.
Gurvich, E. A., 1918, 'Prodarmiya i prodotryady', *Izvestiya*, No. 288, 31 December.
Istoriya Rossii v XIX v., tt. 1–9, Granat, 1907–11, St. Petersburg.
Klyuchevskii, V. O., 1919, *Opyty i issledovaniya*, Moscow.
Klyuchevskii, V. O., 'Proiskhozhdenie krepostnogo prava v Rossii', *Opyty i issledovaniya*. Reprinted in his *Sochineniya*, VII, 1959:170–236.
Klyuchevskii, V. O., 'Russkii rubl' XVI–XVIIIvv.', *Opyty i issledovaniya*. Reprinted in his *Sochineniya*, VII, 1959:237–317.
Kremnev, I. [A. V. Chayanov], 1920, *Puteshestvie moego brata Alekseya v stranu krest'yanskoi utopii*, Moscow.
Ladyzhnikov, I. P., E. F. Rozmirovich (eds.), 1948, *Opisanie rukopisei M. Gor'kogo*, 1, Moscow-Leningrad.

Lappo, I. I., 1894, *Tverskoi uezd v XVI v.*, Moscow.

Larin, Yu. [M. A. Lur'e], 1923, *Voprosy krest'yanskogo khozyaistva*, Moscow.

Lazić, B. M. 1973, *Biographical Dictionary of the Comintern*, Stanford.

Letopis' zhizni i tvorchestva A. M. Gor'kogo, 1959, 1–4, Moscow.

Maslov, P. P., 1906, *Agrarnyi vopros v Rossii*, St. Petersburg.

Maslov, S. L., 1915, *Krest'yanskoe khozyaistvo*, Moscow.

Masanov, I. F., 1956–60, *Slovar' psevdonimov*, I–IV, Moscow.

Milyukov, P. N., 1892, *Spornye voprosy finansovoi istorii Moskovskago gosudarstva*, St. Petersburg.

Nikolai -on [N. F. Danielson], 1893, *Ocherki nashego poreformennago obshchego khozyaistva*, St. Petersburg.

Orwell, G., 1968, *The Collected Essays, Journalism and Letters of George Orwell*, I–IV, London.

Oulanoff, H., 1966, *The Serapion Brothers*, (Slavistic Printings and Reprintings, XLIV), The Hague, Paris.

Ozerov, I. Kh., 1917, *Osnovy finansovoi nauki*, vyp. 1, Moscow.

Pokrovskii, M. N., 1913, *Russkaya istoriya*, tt. I–V, Moscow.

Polnaya entsiklopediya russkago sel'skago khozyaistva, tt. 1–11, 1900–09, St. Petersburg.

Pridorogin, 1896, *Kormovye sredstva*

Rozhkov, N. A., 'Gosudarstvennoe khozyaistvo v Rossii s 60-kh do nachala 90-kh godov', in *Istoriya Rossii v XIXv.*, VI: 69–114.

Rozhkov, N. A., 1899, *Sel'skoe khozyaistvo Moskovskoi Rusi v XVI veke*, Moscow.

Rozhkov, N. A., 1920, 'Narodnoe khozyaistvo Moskovskoi Rusi vo vtoroi polovine XVI v.', *Dela i dni*, I:40–79.

Shane, Alex M., 1968, *The Life and Works of Evgenii Zamyatin*, Berkeley.

Shanin, T. (ed.), 1971, *Peasants and Peasant Societies, selected readings*, Harmondsworth.

Shaw, Nonna D., 1963, 'The only Soviet literary utopia', *The Slavic and East European Journal*, VII, No. 3:279–83.

Shcherbina, F. A., 1900, *Krest'yanskie byudzhety*, Voronezh.

Sobranie Uzakonenii i rasporyazhenii rabochego i krest'yanskogo pravitel'stva.

Solzhenitsyn, A., 1974, *The Gulag Archipelago, 1918–1956* (trans. T. P. Whitney), London.

Sovremennoe sostoyanie l'novodstva.

Statisticheskii Ezhegodnik po Tverskoi gubernii.

Statisticheskii ezhegodnik Rossii, 1904, St. Petersburg.

Statisticheskoe ekonomicheskoe obsledovanie gruntovykh dorog.

Struve, G. P., 1976, 'Ob A. V. Chayanove i ego utopii', *Novoe russkoe slovo*, 31 March: 2 and 4.

Struve, G. P., 1972, *Russian literature under Lenin and Stalin 1917–1953*, London.

Struve, P. B., 1913, *Krepostnoe khozyaistvo*, Moscow.

Vargin, V. N., 1912, *Prostye raschety po organizatsii krest'yanskago khozyaistva*, Moscow.

Veselovskii, S. B. 1915–16, *Soshnoe pis'mo*, I–II, Moscow.

Vladislavlev, I. V. [I. V. Gul'binskii], 1924, *Russkie pisateli*, Moscow.

Volkonskii, N., 'Usloviya pomeshchich'ego khozyaistva pri krepostnom prave', *Trudy Ryazanskoi uchenoi arkhivnoi kommissii za 1897 g.*, XII, vyp. 2 i 3.

Yanson, Yu. E., 1887, *Opyt statisticheskago issledovaniya o krest'yanskikh nadelakh i platezhakh*, St. Petersburg.

Printed in Great Britain by Chapel River Press, Andover, Hants.